JEWISH SOCIA
SOCIALIST HIST

SOCIALIST HISTORY
OCCASIONAL PAPERS SERIES
No. 26

UNION BREAD

BAGELS, PLATZELS AND CHOLLAH:
THE STORY OF THE
LONDON JEWISH BAKERS' UNION

LARRY WAYNE

2009

Published by the
Jewish Socialists' Group
and the Socialist History Society
2009

ISBN 978-0-9555138-3-1

Cover image: Banner of the London Jewish Bakers' Union
Reproduction courtesy of the Jewish Museum, London

Designed and typeset by SHS, 2009
www.socialisthistorysociety.co.uk

Contents

Harry (Larry) Wayne – An Ordinary-Extraordinary Life	 2
Chapter 1. The London Jewish Bakers' union – a triply unique union	 7
Chapter 2. The Beginning	 12
Chapter 3. The International Bakers' Union	 17
Chapter 4. The Campaign against Sunday Baking	 24
Chapter 5, "You Are Our Brothers ... We Wish You Had Not Come"	 32
Chapter 6. The New Century	 42
Chapter 7. 1904: A Momentous Year	 50
Chapter 8. The Court Case 1904	 61
Chapter 9. A Battle on All Fronts	 65
Chapter 10. 1913: "The Ghetto Anticipated Them All"	 76
Chapter 11. 1914-1939	 82
Chapter 12. The Rule Book of 1933	 87
Chapter 13. 1940-1969: Decline and Fall?	 90
Chapter 14. Conditions of Work from 1939 Onwards	 95
Appendix. In a Jewish Bakery	 103
Notes	 105
Suggested further reading	 111

Harry (Larry) Wayne – An Ordinary-Extraordinary Life, 3 December 1914 - 10 January 2008

Harry Wayne was born in the East End of London in the early months of the First World War into a Lithuanian/British Jewish family whose environment and culture was crucial to his formation.

His English-born mother Rachel was taken "back" to Lithuania as a small child, and arrived again on her own in London as a Yiddish speaking 10 year old. Leaving school two years later, her English was fluent and unaccented. Though highly literate in both languages, her relaxation choice was Yiddish, and when she had any time off from rearing eight children in extreme poverty, she read through all the Yiddish translations in the Whitechapel Library's extensive collection of world classics.

His father Louis came from Lithuania to Britain as a baby. At 24 he met the 16 year old Rachel and they were married and parents within twelve months. Louis was a master cobbler, extremely skilled and a ferociously hard worker, but employed in an industry ripe for mechanisation. As a result, by the time Harry was a teenager, his father had entered a long, debilitating and destructive period of unemployment.

Harry always said that when he was a small child, his family were, like most around them, "high day and holy day" Jews, practising, but not fiercely so. However, when he reached eight things changed, and his family became extremely Orthodox. To the end of his days Harry could still daven with the best of them, hurtling through the Hebrew texts he had grown up with. Indeed, living in a Jewish Care home nearly eighty years after he had given up his own religious belief, he would comment acerbically when one of his fellow residents' reciting of the brachas didn't come up to his high standards.

After Jews Free School Harry went to Davenant Foundation Grammar where, by his own admission, he excelled at maths, Latin and anything requiring rote learning! So he was really good at "electricity and magnetism" though never understanding a word while doing it, and forgetting everything as soon as Matriculation exams were over. Yet he was immensely intellectually curious, and intensely intellectually honest. As his doubts about religion grew, he chose a different *shul* each Saturday to see if any had something to offer. At 14 he resisted his mother's attempt to take him out of school and get a job in a shop, and by 18 he had won a place at the London School of Economics to read history.

He had also become a Communist – a very common path then for young Jewish people with a strong sense of justice. Contributing to his passionate love for and protectiveness of his mother was the way she defended him when he was "reported" to his father for selling the *Daily Worker* on a Saturday. When Harry vowed he would leave home if prevented from continuing his Sabbath political activities (though, as he acknowledged later, this was sheer bravado as he had nothing to live on and nowhere to go) his deeply religious mother declared "If he goes, I go". Nobody went.

Though the 1930s LSE that Harry attended was regarded as a radical hotbed, his memories were different. There were some wonderful left wing teachers – particularly Harold Laski – but the great majority of students were very reactionary. And Harry's own experience was defined by his background. As one of a tiny handful of working class university students, he always felt an awkward outsider. Penniless, after having missed a scholarship by a couple of marks, he walked to and from the college each day with not even enough money for bus fares. He hugged the corridor walls trying to be inconspicuous and never once had even a cup of tea in the college canteen – till treated by his older daughter Naomi, who followed him to the LSE thirty six years later.

Harry graduated in the middle of the depression with a non-vocational degree, no job and not a clue what to do next. He took what work he could find, including a stint at the British Tutorial Institutes, a correspondence college. However, that job came to a halt after Harry and friends Harry Roth and Reuben Cohen organised a strike for higher wages. Harry was very proud of his TUC Tolpuddle Medal, awarded for recruiting more than ten new union members, and in later life would laugh, remembering how his boss justified his dismissal as a contribution to intensifying the class struggle!

He then spent three years with the Jewish Refugee Committee, where his abiding memory was the resentment of the middle class German Jews helped by the JRC to resettle, at having to rely on support from working class East Enders with not a penny to their names.

During the Second World War Harry rose to the dizzy rank of Sergeant in the Pay Corps. Though frustrated that, in common with most soldiers, he was supporting the combat troops rather than fighting himself, he was forever grateful that his attempt to be a hero by volunteering for an Allied glider assault on Italy was scuppered by bad eyesight. He would often recall how all those accepted as glider pilots died in the ill-judged campaign.

Post war, Harry worked for UNWRA and finally, in his mid thirties, became a teacher in Sandringham Secondary Modern School in what is now the London Borough of Newham. He would recount the bewilderment of County Hall bureaucrats when he first applied for a job in the old LCC. With an LSE history degree he could have gone anywhere in the teaching profession – they didn't understand why he wanted a secondary modern school in a deprived part of the capital. If not a grammar school, why not a Jewish school, they pressed him. But he held firm to his belief that his place lay with working class kids branded as eleven plus failures – he thought they deserved the best possible education from teachers with the best possible qualifications.

In the late 1940s Harry met fellow Communist and East Ender Lily Bloom at a political meeting. Lily enjoyed describing how, arriving soaking wet from the rain, she had been trying to remove her muddy stockings as surreptitiously as possible when she looked up and found Harry transfixed by the sight. Three years later she married this man whom she always called "Larry", as Communists all called him, after one of his Communist friends said it suited him better!

Harry/Larry and Lily were both committed and very independent minded, deeply worried as early as the late 1940s about stories of Stalinism, in particular Stalinist anti-semitism. While they struggled to believe that the party and movement which they had known as leading the fight against fascism could be anti-semitic, they anguished about the number of Jews falling foul of Socialist regimes in other countries, and the uncritical response of the British Communist Party. Harry pointed out, for example, that "guilty" headlines were already appearing in the *Daily Worker*, well before the notorious Russian Doctors' Trial had even started. Yet, as others who had previously uncritically defended the Soviet Union, fled the British Communist Party after Khrushchev's 1956 speech and the invasion of Hungary in 1957, Harry worked even harder for the cause.

Eventually, it was not events overseas that led Harry to resign in 1957, but his doubt that the British Communist Party would itself democratise. (Though sharing his doubts, Lily stayed a member, convinced in those pre-feminist days, that if she left too, everyone would attribute her decision to him!)

Fewer outside commitments meant Harry could pour his energies into the boys he taught. Today when the pressure is on for *all* children to get "five good GCSEs", it has been largely forgotten that until the 1970s most school leavers – being secondary modern school "graduates" – had no qualifications at all. Harry hated the way 80% of children were written off at eleven, and devoted his teaching career to demonstrating how unjust this was. To put secondary modern boys in for 'O' levels (as they then were) meant a fight with the local authority, and then another struggle to enable them to follow up with 'A' levels. But Harry's battles were vindicated by his students – numbers taking GCEs rose yearly, and only one ('little sod' as Harry called him) ever failed to get a Grade 'A'.

In the early 1970s Harry contracted throat cancer. Though treatment at the Royal Marsden Hospital was successful, he had to retire in 1972, which meant a return to political activism. He fundraised super effectively for Medical Aid for Vietnam (always a great political income generator, he was intensely proud that as Stepney Communist Party branch treasurer, he was the first party officer ever to raise sufficient income for party workers to have paid holidays!) and later he and Lily set up the Redbridge Trade Union and Pensioners Action Group.

Harry's curiosity never left him. When he retired he travelled with Lily to three places he (though not she!) had always wanted to see – the Soviet Union, the United States and Israel. They had a great time, saw amazing things, met wonderful people everywhere they went, and returned with their critical assessments of all three countries (as distinct from their peoples) confirmed. When somebody said to Harry it was too painful even to think about the Soviet Union, he responded that he was tired of avoidance, secrets and lies, and wanted to know *everything*!

Though an atheist since his teens, Harry always saw himself as Jewish. He admitted to irrational food aversions (no pork or shellfish), would challenge anti-semitism wherever he found it, and spoke with the cadences and the occasional Yiddishism of a Whitechapel Jew of his generation. His last political engagement was utterly Jewish – he and Lily were two of the earliest signatories to join up to the campaigning network Jews for Justice for Palestinians when it was formed in 2002, and when too frail to march, indeed, barely able to walk, he took the Tube into central London to stand at the kerbside in solidarity with demonstrators campaigning for the end to occupation and a just Middle East settlement.

Harry came from a large, noisy, intense and talented family, four boys and four girls, and when asked for his happiest memories, said it was growing up with so much love and laughter and family feeling around him. His two elder brothers were keen to get jobs as soon as possible, but his youngest brother followed him to the LSE and became a government statistician, while, at various times, all four of his sisters were teachers.

He left his imprint on his daughters too. Naomi was a trade union officer and later a charity chief executive, while Margaret taught in nursery education, becoming a head teacher in London's East End when only 34 years old. Naomi was previously in the Communist Party in Britain and in Ireland, and is now deeply involved in Jewish campaigning against the Israeli occupation of Palestine, while Margaret has been active in CND, Oxfam and many other voluntary activities.

Most of all, Harry valued his partnership with Lily. Friends and family alike dreaded the moment when one or other would die – though utterly individual, each perfectly complemented the other. As Harry was six years older, everyone assumed he would "go" first, so it was a huge shock when, at 83, Lily was diagnosed with pancreatic cancer and was dead within a week. So close had they been, it was also taken for granted that Harry, like many bereaved widowers would follow soon after. In fact, he lived another five years, still curious, with critical faculties unimpaired, still passionate about theatre and film, struggling on painful feet to central London matinees, still as political as ever.

Fifty years after he had left the Communist Party, he still yearned to make the world a better place and made what contribution he could right up to the end.

Naomi Wayne

Larry Wayne 1914-2008. Picture courtesy of Sid Kaufman

Chapter 1. The London Jewish Bakers' union – a triply unique union

Probably only those whose "way of life is fall'n into the sere, the yellow leaf" will retain fond memories of pre-war days when the fragrant odour of freshly baked bread issued forth from the bakeries of Grodzinski, Kossoff, Rinkoff, Goldring, Bernstein, Ross... Those were the days when every other street in parts of the East End of London had its baker's shop, with bread baked on the premises, its windows and counters piled high with bagels, platzels, rye bread and chollah — the staple food of the residents of Whitechapel, Mile End, the Commercial Road and adjacent squalid, but lively streets. Immigrants forced from Eastern Europe, especially those escaping Tsarist repression, had brought with them not only their traditional way of life, but also the culinary delicacies which helped add flavour to a life which was bleak, bitter and filled with uncertainty.

Today most of those baker's shops are gone forever, with a few exceptions – Rinkoff's in Stepney Green, Kossoff catering for city workers, and Grodzinski, with its score or so of branches – and the products are generally baked in factories rather than in small bakehouses.

A triply unique union

It is remarkable that while a host of professional and amateur historians have studied Jewish history in the modern era,[1] often in the most minute detail, practically nothing has been published on the unique experience of "ethnic" or "national" trade unionism. But while the latest issue of the *Encyclopaedia Judaica* has not a word to say about the Jewish Bakers' Union, the *Jewish Encyclopaedia* of 1906 commented that of all the Jewish Unions "only one has so far become conspicuous - that of the Jewish bakers".[2] This is not to say that Jewish trade unions did not exist before the establishment of the London Jewish Bakers' Union, nor that other nationalities were without their separate unions – there was, for example, a Turkish Tobacco Cutters' Union, which joined the London Trades Council in 1907.[3] The uniqueness of the London Jewish Bakers' Union was that it was one of the last, and certainly the longest-lived, of the specifically religious or ethnic unions in the United Kingdom. It was founded at the end of the 19th century, and survived until 1969. It was unique also in that, for most of its existence, its membership was concentrated in one area of London, Stepney, although later it extended to other areas of East and North London, and in that it organised around the production of a commodity, a specific type of bread or roll, invented on the Continent and produced for a largely immigrant population.

Although in some respects it was a tiny unimportant union, a famous set of names, nationally and internationally renowned, figured in its history: Keir Hardie, first chairman of the Parliamentary Labour Party, John Burns, leader of the dock strike, Herbert Burrows, guiding spirit with Annie Besant behind the Match Girls' Strike, Charlotte Despard, leading suffragette and staunch supporter of a host of progressive causes, and Eleanor Marx, daughter of Karl Marx. Moreover, the union was the plaintiff in a court case of some importance in trade union history.

This pamphlet looks at what the union achieved in its eight decades of history, why it declined and why it finally disappeared.

An oppressed branch of the industrial army

It is one of the ironies of life that the most industrious in society, who do most to provide the essentials of life, are frequently the least rewarded. So it was in the 19th century with the agricultural workers, who provided the raw materials and, in turn, with the bakehouse workers, who created the "staff of life". Despite the difficulties confronting them, the tillers of the soil were driven to combine to improve their lot, and provided the early victims of their oppressors — the Tolpuddle Martyrs. So too, even though they were scattered around small bakehouses, the bakers struggled to combine to improve their pitiful conditions.

In 1847 the Chartist leader, Bronterre O'Brien, referred to the plight of the bakery workers in Manchester and in London, their efforts to reduce their excessive hours of labour, and the appalling conditions they had to endure. In London, for example, journeymen bakers toiled in underground bakehouses, in an over-heated atmosphere, ill-ventilated by night and by day. They worked as much as 20 hours a day, with barely any time to snatch a few mouthfuls of food and drink. O'Brien commented that while trade unionists were combining to reduce hours and to abolish night-work and Sunday baking, by restricting themselves to their immediate demands they could only mitigate the pressure of slavery. He urged them to unite to reform society.[4]

A lengthy article, published in 1850 in *Reynolds Political Instructor* under the name of "Gracchus", was even more revealing about the position of the London journeymen bakers. It referred to a lecture by William Guy, "physician of high standing" who, with the assistance of Mr. Read, Secretary of the Bakers' Society, made a searching and impartial examination into the conditions of journeymen bakers in London. He found that a large proportion worked 18 to 20 hours a day, many at the end of the week for two days in succession. Bakehouse ovens were often underground and subject to flooding. Bakeries were hot and sulphurous, overrun with rats, without ventilation and not uncommonly with a privy in the bakehouse itself. After questioning just over 100 journeymen bakers – just as he had questioned those in other trades – Dr. Guy had "not encountered anywhere a thoroughly healthy worker". Only 14 of the 100 looked tolerably healthy. Compared to dustmen and bricklayers, six times as many bakers were, at first glance, in decidedly bad health. Nearly half of them, Guy considered, were in delicate health and had a sickly look.

In the same issue Gracchus reported that the previous July in the House of Commons, Lord Robert Grosvenor had pleaded for leave to bring in a Bill to regulate working hours in London bakeries, to reduce the hours to 14 a day and do away with night-work. However, the proposal was rejected. Richard Cobden, the great radical and one-time leader of the Anti-Corn Law League, led the opposition to Grosvenor on the principle of perfect freedom for industry. Cobden told the House that Grosvenor's Bill was communistic and that regulating policy was communism. To Gracchus this vaunted freedom meant simply "the liberty to die" more quickly. Gracchus described the London bakers as "one of the most useful and most oppressed branches of the industrial army", and remarked that while "we cannot say we have much hope of their success with the present Parliament, we nevertheless recommend them to persevere".[5]

For all their perseverance, their pleas and their efforts to organise, the lot of the bakery workers, especially in London, did not improve over the succeeding decades. Thus in 1866 *The Working Man*, published in London, contained an article luridly headed "Grind his bones to make my bread". The writer charged that the journeyman baker's life is "ground out of him" by hard work. When others are in the prime of health and strength, he is a "decrepid" man, whom "consumption and innumerable other ills mark for their own". He cited the story of George Spriggs, journeyman baker, one of many thousands similarly situated, who died at the age of 54 in a bakehouse in Cowcross Street. Working from five every afternoon till eight or nine every morning, he was at liberty to lie down for a short time, while the oven was getting hot, on a sack in the corner of the bakehouse with black beetles running over him. Spriggs then had to go out for three or four hours delivering bread carrying a heavy basket or pushing a barrow. When he reached home at two o'clock in the afternoon, he was so exhausted by his 21 hours of labour that he laid down to rest too weary even to undress.[6]

The Working Man, which aimed "to assist in the promotion of the intellectual, social and industrial welfare of the various classes of workers whether by hand or brain", in a later issue stressed the excessively long hours (12-18) and the unhealthy character of the places in which the journeyman baker performed his tasks. "The bakehouse is often made to serve the purpose of workshop, living-room and bedroom all combined" and "there are many journeymen bakers who have scarcely ever known what it is to sleep in a bed". Many of the bakers came from Germany, "attracted to the country by the hope of higher rates of wages than was procurable in their own". Worn out before their time "consumption and diseases of the lung prevailed to a frightful extent among them, and the spectacle of an aged journeyman baker is somewhat rare". While a few master bakers had tried to improve conditions — there were some large well-ventilated bakehouses where night-work was at a minimum — for most the only remedy was that the public should refuse to deal with bakeries where such appalling conditions prevailed.[7]

The desperate plight of the workers in the baking industry led to the formation in 1861 of the Amalgamated Union of Operative Bakers and Confectioners of Great Britain and Ireland (AUOB). In 1880 the AUOB London District Board issued an Address and Platform to the journeymen bakers of London, which explained the reasons for the evil situation in the trade, and set out the aims of the union and some of its successes. The language of this address may seem very colourful or extravagant, but it reflected the deep-seated emotions of men suffering intolerable privations. The union recognised that it is "the isolation and indifference of journeymen bakers which places them in such a helpless condition ... when a baker is constantly employed he barely receives sufficient to keep himself or those who may be depending on him in health and strength and is generally verging towards a premature grave or an English workhouse". The union expressed a sense of humiliation in that "whilst other industrial bodies have reduced their hours of labour to about 52 or 54 per week, yet the generality of bakers are working 80 or 100 hours per week".

In its address, the union was encouraged by the fact that about 800 new members had recently joined. It noted the union's exposure of "a number of the wretched dens in which the journeymen have to spend the greater portion of their existence and ... its prevention of the building of a great number of underground bakehouses". The union was constantly complaining about Sunday baking, and it was proud to point out that about 30 masters had been summonsed for this practice. The address did not contend "every employer is necessarily a monster in human form", but it insisted that "unless there is a strong union ... those who actually create all the wealth become a prey to every vulture who chooses to drain them of their life's blood". Against "the monstrous prevailing custom which allows an employer the right to exact over 24 hours at a stretch", the union advocated "that no journeyman shall work more than 10 hours a day or 60 hours a week". It emphasised that "disorganized labour can never obtain its just and natural share of the profits it produces".

Chapter 2. The Beginning

Jews first entered England after the Norman Conquest. Edward I expelled them in 1290 with considerable cruelty. Not till the 16th century did any return – and then not openly. In 1656 Cromwell finally permitted Jewry to re-establish itself in England. By 1850, as a result of immigration from Holland, Germany, and other European countries, there were 35,000 Jews in Britain, about half of them in London. The transition from predominantly Dutch and German immigration to immigration from Eastern Europe occurred between 1865 and 1875.

The year 1881 brought great changes: Alexander II of Russia was assassinated, and this provided an excuse to launch attacks upon the Jews. The first peak of emigration from Eastern Europe took place in 1881 and 1882. Anti-Semitic riots and the anti-Jewish May Laws of 1882 in the Tsarist Empire were a powerful stimulus driving the Jews westwards. The general economic conditions of Jewry in Russia also exerted constant pressure on the mass of the poverty-stricken Jewish people to leave for lands which not only were more tolerant, but where Jews could hope for something better than a mere hand-to-mouth existence.

The period of mass Jewish immigration coincided with the appearance of the New Unionism and the remarkable expansion of British trade unionism, and this growth was bound to have some effect among the Jewish working population. The first Jewish trade union in Britain was a union of tailors formed in 1874. It had 72 members and lasted only a few weeks.[1]

From the end of the 1880s to the first decade of the 20th century small unions were constantly rising and falling, forming and dissolving, splitting and reuniting. In the 1890s there were 15 Jewish unions in the clothing trade and 12 in the boot and shoe trades.[2] Despite their special difficulties, Jewish bakers soon began to play their own part in the trade union movement. When precisely and why the Jewish Bakers' Union finally adopted their eventual name as the London Jewish Bakers' Union is not clear. It was not till 1912 that the union is called the London Jewish Bakers' Union in the *Jewish Year Book*. But already in 1909, when the union applied for affiliation to the General Federation of Trade Unions and to the London Trades Council, it was referred to as the London Jewish Bakers' Union.[3]

We do not know why the union changed its name. It is probable that its original name, International Bakers' Union, was adopted because its membership originated from so many different countries — Poland, the Russian Empire, Holland, and England itself.

It seems there were no strict conditions for joining the union. From the testimony of most of the former union members I have been able to question, there was no apprenticeship. Many who entered were already bakers when they first arrived in England – like Mr. Grodzinski, founder of the largest chain of Jewish bakers' shops.[4] Some were the sons of bakers. Morris Cohen, for example, a member of the union from the early 1920s till its dissolution, started work in his father's bakery in Highbury (his father had earlier had a baker's shop in East London) and was subsequently employed in his uncle's bakery in Hanbury Street, East London. Yet others entered the profession by chance. For example, according to Mr. Cohen, homeless immigrants would often throw themselves on the mercy of a kindly baker, and would be allowed to sleep in the bakery, sheltering from the bitter winds of the cold London night. Sleeping there close to the ovens they had opportunities – night baking was commonplace – to learn the craft of baking and thereby gain entry into the trade.

First Stirrings

In 1888 came the first signs of a stirring of revolt among Jewish bakers. An article signed "captious critic" in the *Journeymen Bakers Magazine* (*JBM*), the organ of the AUOB, reported that about 300 Jewish bakers in the East End of London had struck a few days previously. "These people were not organized in any way whatever, and, of course, the affair ended in 'a fizzle', most of the poor slaves going back with an 'Irishman's rise'. I hear (and this in a country which professes a religion and a code of morals founded by a Jew) that the Jewish bakers work for four or five shillings per week. Jobbers have to work from 3pm on Thursdays till 6pm Fridays (27 hours) for three shillings".[5]

The AUOB London District Board secretary was astonished "that men so oppressed as they appeared to be would never amalgamate, although they had many times been invited", and the London District Board unanimously resolved "that our hearty sympathy be extended to them in their struggle to improve their miserable condition".[6]

Despite its failure it was a remarkable achievement to have persuaded a comparatively large body of men to take such action, when they were employed in a host of tiny bakehouses and were so easily subject to victimisation. In fact, judging from the report on the strike in the Yiddish anarchist weekly, *Arbeter Fraynd*,[7] it is almost certain the action was spontaneous and unorganised, and may well have been sparked off by an incident in one bakehouse, even though its root causes were deep-seated. According to the writer, on the previous Monday a large crowd in working clothes and covered in white flour flocked through Whitechapel, stopping outside each bakery, appealing — with seemingly immediate success — to the workers to come out. The local German bakery workers provided encouragement.

Working conditions were deplorable in every respect, but this action was primarily for a reduction in hours. With many "greenhorns" (recent immigrants) still working, the strike was doomed to failure. *Arbeter Fraynd* stressed that the bakehouse of the well-known philanthropist baker Simon Cohen, or Simcha Becker as he was commonly called, was unaffected by the strike, because, the paper stingingly remarked, "in his 'shtibl' (a room used as a synagogue) and bakehouse he has 'layabouts' whom he can recruit". Attacking the exploiting master bakers the paper asked, "How long will sweating parasites ride on the worker's back and laugh in his face?" As long as the workers are isolated the "vampire" masters will retain power, and therefore the *Arbeter Fraynd* called on all workers to unite and organise.

The AUOB were obviously concerned to assist their Jewish fellow workers. A later issue of the *Journeymen Bakers Magazine* reported that the general secretary, Mr. Jenkins, with other members visited Jewish bakers in the East End. Thanks especially to the indefatigable efforts of Jacob Jung, the chairman of the German branch of the AUOB, a new branch, No. 21 London Branch of the AUOB, had been set up consisting solely of Jewish bakers. Over 30 members had already been made, and more names were being given in and, it was hoped, "that in a very short time the Sunday baking in the East (End) will gradually be blotted out by means of the growing strength of the Union".[8] Alas for the AUOB, this hope was doomed to be disappointed — as Jewish bakers were closed on Saturday, the Jewish Sabbath, both Jewish employers and journeymen bakers assumed it was acceptable, at a time when the six-day week was taken for granted, that Sunday was a working day.

Mr Jenkins and other leading members of the AUOB, speaking in English, pointed out the benefits of combining together. The meeting continued in the German language; and many of those present "told their pitiful tales of woe and misery". The *Journeymen*

Bakers Magazine was impressed by the occasion, concluding these "Hebrews — Polish, Russian and German Jews — have accomplished a great deal by means of the circulation of a small paper of their own, the *Workman's Friend*". The Jewish bakers "anticipate in the near future a change in their conditions for the better". This optimism, unfortunately, was to prove ill-founded.

The Jewish branch met at the "Duke of Gloster" (sic) in New Road E1, and its secretary was E. Goldberg who lived at 9 Paternoster Row, Brushfield Street, E1. Its stated membership in November 1888 was 32. This was not to be sneered at — the London No. 27 branch for example, had 26 members, and the Cheltenham branch had only two members — and by February 1889 the membership of the Jewish branch had increased by two. But after May 1889 there was no further mention in the magazine's report of branch activities, nor was there any report of the Jewish branch making any contribution to AUOB. The branch had probably collapsed, and perhaps it is not surprising, bearing in mind the report at the end of 1888 that "the position of the journeyman baker is as bad, if not worse, than in any previous period during the last 20 years" and that "conditions are a shame and disgrace to a wealthy Christian nation".[9]

However, this apathy was not long lasting. The bakers, both Jewish and non-Jewish, were affected by the ferment among the workers at large, in particular by the success of the dockers' strike of 1889. In October 1889 the union magazine reported a meeting held in Hyde Park under the auspices of the AUOB. The crowd of about 10,000 was addressed by the legendary John Burns who, describing the appalling conditions endured by the bakers, who worked sometimes over 100 hours a week in "pig sties", moved the limitation of bakers' hours to 60 a week.

In the next issue of *Journeymen Bakers Magazine*, the No. 21 London branch, the "Hebrew branch", reappeared. It also reported that notices had been sent to all London AUOB members instructing them to inform their employers that they would cease work on 9 November if their demands for a shorter working week were not granted.[10] The last issue for 1889 reported that the operative bakers had been successful in winning the 10 hour system in London, though some master bakers were breaking the agreement. To celebrate the bakers' triumph a march of about 4,000, of whom it appears only a quarter were actually bakers, took place, headed by Hoxton Town Band. The men displayed insignia — small loaves and bakers' peels — and wore white aprons and linen jackets. In the midst of the march there was a contingent from the "Hebrew branch" bearing aloft a banner, and on the front of their flag the motto "Unity is Strength" and the intimation that they were "sweated victims and we demand our rights".[11]

The revived militancy of the Jewish bakers was part of a wider movement. A meeting of representatives of various trade unions was held at the International Workingmen's Educational Club in Berner Street, Commercial Road, with the object of the federation of all classes of Jewish workers in the East End of London. Mr. Goldstein of the Pressers' Union pointed to the success of the recent tailors' strike, involving thousands of Jewish tailors, as an example of the value of combination. He urged the audience to recognise the virtue of federation, in that one trade in difficulty could gain moral and financial support from others. Another speaker, Woolf Wess, anarchist and secretary of the strike committee, championed the establishment of a Jewish trades council, because many Jewish workers did not understand English and it was futile therefore to ask them to join an English trades council.[12]

In 1890, for the first time, the *Journeymen Bakers Magazine* mentioned entrance fees, contributions totalling £17 and levies of £2 16s. 0d from the No. 21 branch.[13] Alas, the branch lacked stability. By the end of the year it had seemingly collapsed again, for while the magazine regularly listed its branches, the name and members of the Jewish branch no longer featured.

In January 1891, the *Jewish Chronicle* responded to those who criticised the weakness of trade unionism among Jewish workers, "the reproach that he (the Jewish workman) has a constitutional dislike for combination can hardly be levelled at him any longer". It added, "he is quite sufficiently adept at strikes", continued, "nor does the Jewish workman refuse his sympathy to combination outside his own trade. The Jews were among the first to contribute to the dockers' strike fund", and concluded, "nothing but mutual benefit can result from closer relations between Jew and Gentile in the labour world".[14] However it is clear from all the evidence that as far as Jewish journeymen bakers were concerned, trade unionism was at a low ebb.

Chapter 3. The International Bakers' Union

A period of inactivity was followed by renewed struggle in 1893. The *Journeymen Bakers Magazine* reported: "After two attempts by the Amalgamated Union to organize the Jew bakers, which both proved failures, they have made another start to organize, this time called the International Bakers' Union". A procession was followed by a mass meeting in Buck's Row (now Durward Street), Whitechapel. After opening the meeting, at the insistence of some of the Jews on the platform, Jacob Jung, secretary of the German branch of the National Union, addressed the gathering. Although he applauded their efforts to organise themselves and to "better their miserable existence" he disapproved of the demand by the chairman of the meeting for a 12-hour day, "when the AUOB have 10 hours on their flag".[1]

Reynolds News also covered the revived efforts of the Jewish bakers, reporting two meetings on the front page and page three.[2] In the afternoon at Buck's Row Mr. C. Guilaroff presided. Addressing the audience in Yiddish, he pointed out the advantages of union and the need to strengthen the International Bakers' Union. He was followed by Keir Hardie who congratulated the Jewish Bakers' Union on being the first in the country to adopt the union label for its goods (a label indicating that the bread was baked by union labour, to be stuck on each loaf). He passionately inveighed against the distressing working conditions of the Jewish journeymen bakers. Consumers as well as producers would suffer, if nothing were done to end the unhealthy conditions of bread baking, which could lead to the spread of disease. He believed the County Council should establish municipal bakeries, and trusted that if the employers refused to adopt the union label, the men would take matters into their own hands and establish their own bakeries - an interesting suggestion which was to be taken up in the following year. That evening, a mass meeting of East End Jewish workers at St. Augustine's Church Hall appealed "to all Jewish trade unionists to assist and support the International Bakers' Union by refusing to eat bread unless the union sign be upon it".

About two months later both the *Jewish Chronicle* and *Reynolds News* reported the critical situation in the Jewish baking trade, when an extremely unusual, if not unique event in the annals of both trade unionism and the Beth Din occurred. Mr. Guilaroff, secretary of the International Bakers' Union, led a deputation to Finsbury Square, where in the austere and sombre offices of the

Beth Din he appeared before Dr. Hermann Adler, the Chief Rabbi, who was flanked by Dayanim (authorities on Jewish law), to appeal for the powerful assistance of the Chief Rabbi to alleviate the conditions endured by the Jewish bakery workers, who were often compelled to work seven days a week.

Reynolds News commented, "The action taken by the Jewish bakers to bring the influence of the Chief Rabbi to bear on the sweating which goes on in East End bakehouses may have more important consequences than the promoters imagine. There are hundreds – nay thousands – of bakehouses in the Metropolis where hours are as long and the sanitary conditions as bad as those kept by Jews. The men in the baking trade are about the most helpless of all workingmen. Their union is not strong, their wages are small, their hours are twice as long as they ought to be, and the dens in which they work, in a state of semi-nudity, are a disgrace to civilisation. The Chief Rabbi, Dr. Adler, has promised to confer with Mr. S. Montagu MP, on the subject, and if a movement is once started to benefit Jewish bakers and to improve Jewish bakehouses, English bakers and bakehouses will be sure to benefit thereby".[3] Alas, the Chief Rabbi, while expressing his sympathy, and while disturbed by the men's enforced desecration of the Sabbath, was not yet ready to assume the role of a Cardinal Manning, and the pitiless exploitation of Jewish bakers continued unabated.

The union had wished to issue a label under the authority of the Chief Rabbi, to be stuck on every loaf of bread from those employers who agreed to the following conditions: (i) none but union men to be employed (ii) working hours to be 12 a day (iii) no work to be done on Saturday (iv) abolition of overtime, except one hour a day when it is necessary to finish the work in hand. The Chief Rabbi's response was "I cannot favour the use of such a label as proposed as we cannot mix up religious with social questions".[4]

This was a blow to the Jewish journeymen bakers, and in the correspondence column of the *Jewish Chronicle* there is a letter written as much in sorrow as in anger which comments, "Our Chief Rabbi seems to imagine ... that his sphere of influence should be confined to mitigating the religious difficulties of the poor bakers, leaving alone their social difficulties except in so far as these affect their religion. This is to my mind a grievous error ... It is surely the very highest function of the Rabbinate to assuage the burdens of his people".[5]

A further blow was dealt to Jewish trade unionists in the East End when the Home Office rejected a request made by the International Bakers' Union and the United Ladies' Tailors and Mantle Makers for a Jewish inspector of workshops, specially for the East End of London.[6] Similarly, in response to press reports of insanitary conditions in Whitechapel bakeries, the chairman of the Whitechapel sanitary district claimed that of 76 registered bakeries in the district only two failed fully to meet the requirements of the medical officer of health.[7] It was hardly surprising that the Jewish journeymen bakers were unable to move the authorities – the native journeymen bakers were equally ineffective.

The labour leader John Burns, who maintained a keen interest in the baking industry ever since he had worked in a bakehouse as a lad, stressed the intolerable conditions of the bakers,[8] and John Jenkins, the secretary of the AUOB, described the conditions of the industry as worse than those of any skilled industry, but without result.[9] The abysmal conditions in the baking industry, especially in London, continued unchanged. Indeed, in one case reported in the AUOB journal in 1894, the coroner blamed the outrageous conditions in the trade as contributing to the death of a journeyman baker.

The 1890s: Conditions worse than slavery

In the 1890s Charles Booth's monumental *Life and Labour of the People of London* appeared. Volume VII, published in 1896, contained a section describing how bread is made, and giving detailed information on hours of work, wages, sanitary conditions, etc. in the baking industry, as well as facts about trade unions connected with the bread baking industry.

Only about 2,300 bakers in London were members of their trade societies — little more than 20%. Meanwhile in London there were over 500 members linked in the Master Bakers' Protection Society. The weakness of workers' organisation in the face of a strong employers' organisation was undoubtedly responsible in part for the wretched conditions. Relations between masters and men were not cordial, and the masters did not adhere to the agreement for a 60-hour week made after the 1889 strike.

According to returns from 17 bakeries employing 1,016 persons, 58% earned less than 30 shillings a week while the rest earned 30 shillings a week or more. However, most employers gave no information about earnings, which suggests that wages were in fact generally lower.

As for conditions, Booth wrote that, "in London and also in many provincial towns the baker of bread turns night into day. He works for long hours in an almost tropical temperature and inhales the gas-laden air of a bakehouse, often, though not always, small and ill-ventilated and very generally based below the level of the ground". Indeed, in a speech in Hyde Park on 22 March 1896, John Burns charged that London bakery workers endured conditions worse than slavery.[10]

The AUOB gave sick and death benefits, and had a separate optional fund for unemployment benefit. The union for the Jewish bakers gave sick pay and strike and lockout pay, but did not give unemployment benefit. The International Bakers' Union subscription was 6d per week, and members received 12s. a week when sick or on strike. According to Booth, the International Bakers' Union was established in 1890, and had 130 members in 1896. The *Journeymen Bakers Magazine*, however, first mentioned the name only in 1893.

Even when the trade unions had won improvements, these were often whittled away or agreements were simply ignored. So, as Booth observed, "journeymen bakers finding the conditions under which they worked very hard, and having, as it seems, great difficulty in amending them by combination among themselves, turned to the legislature for assistance. They demand the stringent inspection of all bakehouses, and the closing of those which are below the level of the ground. They also ask for the abolition of night work and Sunday work and for the establishment by law of an eight-hour day".

The Co-operative Idea

In the latter part of 1894 there was a remarkable development in the history of Jewish bakery workers, which even got lengthy coverage in the national press. The *Westminster Gazette*[11] published an article - reprinted later in the *Jewish Chronicle* - headed "To kill the Bakehouse Scandal" and sub-headed "Extraordinary demonstration in the East End",.

It is worth citing in full:

> One of the latest surprises in connection with the rapid advance of the Labour movement comes in the shape of a co-operative bakery just opened at 52 Brushfield Street, Spitalfields, founded by and under the control of Hebrew United Trade Organisations. A very crowded meeting was held at Christchurch Hall, Spitalfields,

for the purpose of announcing the formal opening of the shop on the following morning.

The speakers, consisting of representatives from the Hebrew Branch Alliance Cabinet Makers' Society, United Cap Makers, International Bakers' Union, Independent Tailors', Pressers' and Machinists' Union and Boot and Shoe Operatives (Hebrew Branch) were all enthusiastic about the new undertaking which was declared to be a most formidable weapon against the sweating employer, as well as a crushing reply to the false charges brought against the Jewish worker as to backwardness in trade unionism.

From early morning on the Sunday Jewish workers were streaming from all quarters inhabited by them in the direction of the new cooperative shop, while many well-known officials and organizers among the Hebrew workers from diverse trades were seen wheeling about barrows loaded with the "Union Bread", each loaf properly labelled and supplied to the grocers, restaurant keepers and others who have already pledged themselves to patronise "the Union Bread" and no other.

By 10.30 the crowd surrounding the premises numbered some thousands, all spirited and enthusiastic for the new launch upon the troubled waters of the Labour Sea. Mr. Levin of the Tailors' Union, in addressing the crowd from a chair said the object of the co-operation was not only to afford an effective weapon to fight the employers, but also to supply the trade unionists with wholesome and healthy bread baked under proper and sanitary conditions.

It was a pitiful sight to see the joy with which all hearts were filled, especially those engaged in the baking industry. To them who have been accustomed to toil under ground for eighteen, twenty or sometimes twenty-four hours at a stretch at a scant wage of from twelve shillings to twenty five shillings a week, this means quite a revolution.

The speeches over, the band struck up the *Marseillaise*, while the doors of the shop opened amid vociferous cheers from the crowd. Then all the bakers came out dressed in white hats, shirts and aprons, carrying a large cake on a pole and headed by banners from the various trade unions and two bands. The crowd formed a procession in the midst of which was a cartload of new bread and marched through various streets inhabited by Jews, meeting everywhere with much sympathy.

Arriving by one o'clock at Buck's Row a most enthusiastic meeting was held. At half-past two the enthusiastic trade unionists again reformed in procession and accompanied by the two bands marched through the other localities, arriving at the shop by four, where they broke up after giving many hearty cheers for the Co-operation and the Union Bread and groans for the sweating masters.

In another lengthy column "Things to think about" written by the "T. U. Magid" in the *Jewish World* (a Magid is Hebrew for a teacher or preacher) it described how the Jewish Co-operative Bakery "is besieged" every morning by women to obtain the pure bread made in the eight-hour system. As a result of such a great demand for this union bread the bakery had to be worked day and night with three shifts of men. There was even talk of purchasing another bakery to absorb all the union men in their own shops.

Since the opening of the bakery the Jewish master bakers had been having nightly meetings to discuss how to "break" the men up. When the masters reduced the price of bread, the co-operative adopted the novel expedient of *raising* their prices by a farthing a loaf, "and the fun of all this is that the women are paying this higher price instead of going to the cheaper shops". The writer felt that even if the masters gave their bread away for nothing, Jewish trade unionists would not forsake the "Co-operative Bakery".[12]

This optimism was misplaced. The co-operative baker must have collapsed soon thereafter, because neither in 1895, nor in subsequent years, did *Kelly's Postal Directory* (London) refer to any bakery at 52 Brushfield Street, despite the fact that the premises had certainly been used as a bakery since the 1840s. The local directory next referred to those premises in 1900, when a paper merchant took over the shop.

How and why this widely acclaimed experiment failed remains a mystery. The co-operative bakery's closure was neither explained nor even mentioned in the trade papers, trade union papers, or the local and national press. But failure did not deter the union, and within less than three years it embarked upon a similar venture.

Early in January 1897 International Bakers' Union announced it would open a co-operative bakery in Old Montagu Street, E1, that the secretary had been visiting the various unions asking for support and that he had been meeting with signal success.[13] The *Jewish Chronicle*'s labour movement correspondent wrote: "It was opened not in opposition to the masters, but in order to provide employment for some of their members who were out of work". Competition had reduced the price to a level — 4d — at which it was impossible to make a profit. The article continued, "I have been over the Co-operative Bakery paying a surprise visit, and must say that it contrasts favourably as regards cleanliness and general arrangements with many that have been described".[14]

A week later the correspondent wrote, "I am informed that the business at the Jewish Union Co-operative Bakery is very brisk, so much so that they are unable to satisfy the demands made. It is intended as soon as possible to open another bakery on the same principle". Cut-throat competition developed with the master bakers, but within a short time the co-operative, which had started with a capital of £53 raised by members' levies, had made a profit of £25.[15] Soon, thanks to a sympathiser who had undertaken to advance the co-operative £100 if necessary, the International Bakers' Union announced that it would be opening another co-operative bakery.[16]

A fortnight later the *Jewish Chronicle* published a long letter from James Leverson depicting the "dangerous and degrading" conditions suffered by the Jewish journeymen bakers and appealing for support for the development of the co-operative movement which was then only employing seven men. "They seek no eleemosynary aid and do not desire to monopolise the trade, but believe that by the establishment of the bakery in question they can demonstrate to the masters that the hours of labour can be reduced profitably, and induce them to do so through fear of competition in the same manner as the establishment of industrial dwellings has improved the conditions of workingmen's lodgings.... A very moderate sum would be required for the present purpose....and thereby release these poor workmen from such a revolting state of misery".

However within a few months the co-operative bakery, though still in existence, was merely employing five or six men.[17] Support was plainly flagging, there were fewer customers, and it looked as if the venture might fail. "It would certainly not be to the credit of the Jewish workmen if they allowed their comrades to fail in this undertaking".[18] The end was not long in coming "owing to the many bad debts. A sum of £35 is outstanding and the union's funds being insufficient to meet this deficit the bakery had to be given up. This is the second time that a union bakery has come to grief."[19]

Once again there was no serious attempt to analyse why the enterprise failed, but the union was undeterred. There would be further attempts to establish co-operative bakeries in the 20th century.

Chapter 4. The Campaign against Sunday Baking

The AUOB's campaign to use the law against Sunday work began in earnest in 1896. The union journal warned that "trouble is brewing in the trade", and attacked the small German bakers "who have multiplied enormously in the last twenty years" as the worst offenders. It accused them of having long monopolised the East London business and of "spreading like locusts or Australian rabbits, ubiquitously and irresistibly". The German bakers were charged with "sweating their employees, who were mostly their own countrymen, to an extent unparalleled in any other industry".[1] Despite this onslaught upon the German bakers, when the AUOB did swing into action it was against the Jewish bakers, most of whom were not German, that legal measures were taken. Following a complaint brought on behalf of the AUOB, Julius Louis Meek, a baker of 39 Broad Street, Golden Square, was taken to Court and fined 10s for baking on a Sunday.[2]

The case was based on law dating back to the reign of George IV, which prohibited the baking of bread on a Sunday. The *Jewish Chronicle* devoted a great deal of space to this matter in its "Notes of the Week". It noted the magistrate's remark that when the law was framed there were so few Jewish bakers that it never occurred to those responsible for the Act of 1822 to make exceptions for Jewish bakers. The paper agreed that the law had to be obeyed, but argued it was necessary to agitate constitutionally for repeal, and proposed that Jewish bakers should combine to bring their grievances before Jewish MPs and the Board of Deputies. "There are now about sixty Jewish bakeries in London, employing about 150 Jewish journeymen." All kept the Jewish Sabbath and were therefore unable to bake bread from Friday to Monday. So that Jewish bakers should not be forced to open their bakehouses on the Sabbath "supplanting Jewish by non-Jewish labour", the paper urged that "steps should be taken to promote the passage of a Bill in Parliament assimilating the law relating to bakehouses to the Factory and Workshops Act of 1878, section 51, which allows Jewish employers of labour not working on the Jewish Sabbath to avail themselves of Jewish labour for half a day on Sunday."

From then on the columns of the *Jewish Chronicle* and of the *Journeymen Bakers Magazine* were filled with charges and countercharges. Some non-Jewish AUOB members insisted that Jewish bakers were not entitled to discrimination in their favour and were subject to the law of the land like all bakers, while Jewish bakers would imply or sometimes openly state that non-Jewish bakers were being unreasonable or frankly anti-Semitic.

Simon Cohen of 32 Church Lane, E1 published a letter in which he referred to the "revival of an old grievance emanating from the German Christian bakers with the intention of summoning every Jewish master for baking on Saturday nights and Sunday morning". He recalled that 15 years previously, he had been summonsed to Worship Street Police Court in a similar case. On that occasion, he had sought help from several MPs, Lord Rothschild, the late Chief Rabbi, and Lord Beaconsfield. "They wrote to the presiding magistrate and the result was the case was dismissed, he stating that it was a matter for parliament to deal with".[3]

But history was not to repeat itself so favourably. In the very week that this letter appeared Simon Cohen was prosecuted at Marlborough Street Police Court for Sunday baking, and was fined 10s plus costs. Cohen, or Simcha Becker as he was known, was a devout Jewish baker. He was one of the most famous of the Jewish master bakers of the period. He provided assistance to his less fortunate co-religionists who had fled from Tsarist tyranny, by opening a shelter for immigrants in Church Lane in the East End of London. Certain wealthy members of the Jewish community, in particular Frederick Mocatta and Lionel Alexander, described these premises as unhealthy and succeeded in getting them closed. Their real motive was probably a fear that such shelters would attract helpless foreigners to this country. Many native Jews were worried about the influx of immigrants. Protest against the closure of this refuge led other wealthy Jews to open the Poor Jews' Temporary Shelter in October 1885, mainly to receive new immigrants. It continued in existence until the 1980s.[4]

At the AUOB London District Board's monthly meeting on 3 September 1896, a letter from the labour leader and MP John Burns to John Jenkins, General Secretary of the union, was read out: "I trust you will keep a sharp eye on this Jewish agitation for Sunday baking ... there will be an attempt ultimately for religious reasons to break up the six-day working week. The East End Jew middleman has done enough harm already. Don't, if prompt action will stop him, let him revive Sunday work". Following this the members agreed that a deputation of delegates approach the masters on the matter.[5]

When the Jewish master bakers learned of this letter they were indignant, and the following issue of the *Jewish Chronicle* announced that they had formed themselves, under the leadership of the prominent Jewish baker brothers, T. and J. Bonn, into the Hebrew Master Bakers' Association. [6]

Meanwhile, the *Journeymen Bakers Magazine* for October 1896 carried a copy of a statement from the trade paper *The British and Foreign Confectioner and Baker* headed "Six days shalt thou labour". This criticised *Reynolds News* for protesting against the action of the Bakers' Union in causing certain Jewish bakers to be summonsed for baking bread on Sunday.

"*Reynolds* is not interested in arguments that Jews do not bake on the Sabbath. What *Reynolds* objects to is that under an obsolete and persecuting Act of Parliament any person or body of men should be guilty of such acts of persecution and intolerance as are these Sunday prosecutions." *The British and Foreign Confectioner and Baker*, however, argued: "It will be a sorry day for working bakers and not a good one for master bakers either, when firms, Jewish or other, are allowed to bake on Sunday ... If Jewish bakers employ none but Jews and bake for none other than Jews and refrain from baking on the Jewish Sabbath, they might be allowed to bake on Sunday; but under other circumstances they must not be allowed to make their faith an excuse for instituting a seven working days week, nor can they be allowed to create a Sunday trade in bread to the detriment of bakers who do not want to start such practices .... Not one man in ten who works on Sundays does it willingly".

Meanwhile the Jewish master bakers reacted to the prosecutions and resolved to petition Parliament to amend the law so that Jews who do not work on their own Sabbath should be free to work on Sunday. They clearly had a great degree of sympathy — influential figures like Lord Salisbury, Lord Rosebery and the Bishop of London supported the campaign.[7] Even the Archbishop of Canterbury expressed regret that prosecutions were being instituted.[8]

The Hebrew Master Bakers' Association also enlisted the aid of the Jewish Board of Deputies. Sir Samuel Montagu was authorised by the Board to interview the Home Secretary with regard to the grievances of the Jewish bakers. The master bakers made it clear that any member who baked on both Saturday and Sunday would not receive the support of the Association.[9]

In a riposte to the Jewish master bakers' campaign "to get the present laws repealed", the secretary of the AUOB urged his members to contact MPs and to "see that they did not allow 60 Jewish master bakers and some 180 men to prevent thousands of master bakers and journeymen from being deprived of their day of rest".[10]

To be fair to the AUOB secretary, John Jenkins, he admitted that non-Jewish as well as Jewish bakers were working seven days a week, and he was prepared to take action, including court prosecutions. Nevertheless, it was Jewish bakers who especially aroused the ire of the non-Jewish bakers, both masters and journeymen. As one of the speakers at a meeting of the London master bakers remarked: "If the Jew sought the hospitality of our shores, he should do his best to conform to the good usages of the place he has adopted for his living and livelihood".[11] And at a meeting of the Master Bakers' Protection Society in the same month, John Jenkins tried to "enlist sympathy and assistance ...to prevent Sunday working by Jews", pointing out that the union's operatives had "prosecuted those who broke the law but they found it a costly undertaking".[12]

As the *Jewish Chronicle* declared, "it seems that the Christian bakers have declared war to the knife with the Jewish bakers" and the London Master Bakers' Association had succeeded in getting the backing of the Bakery, Biscuit Baking and Confectionery Trade Section of the London Chamber of Commerce against any attempt to secure the legalisation of Sunday baking.[13]

Throughout 1897 Sunday baking remained a burning issue, and a full-page article: "The Sunday Baking Question — a retrospect" was devoted to the whole matter in the *Jewish Chronicle* of 30 April 1897.

The Bread Act, in so far as it related to London, had been passed in 1822, and was extended to the rest of the country in 1836, but there had been no prosecutions until 1863, and these had been trivial. When summonses were taken out in January and February 1876 the *Daily Telegraph* had carried a leading article commenting "If it be wicked to bake a roll or fancy loaf on a Sunday morning, is it not equally naughty to grant the hospitality of the oven to an indefinite number of shoulders of mutton and ribs of beef with puddings or potatoes underneath, which are carried to the bakehouse even while the church bells are ringing, and at 1 p.m., just as the congregation are issuing from their diverse places of worship, are reclaimed and borne away in triumph to the abodes of those whose lot it is to labour?"

The retrospect went on to complain that, after summonses had been issued by the Christian bakers, the *Bakers Record* had insulted the Jews in a leading article on 31 July 1896 which asserted: "We know a Sunday campaign in Middlesex Street among the Jews means to be hooted with vile epithets to be branded as common informers ... Formerly we cruelly persecuted the Jews, now we are excessively tolerant and rather than interfere with his trade proclivities on the Sabbath (i.e. Sunday) Christian operatives are yoked to a week of 7 days slavery".

The *Jewish Chronicle* in retrospect noted that the AUOB had been actively instituting summonses. As many as 40 (according to a report of the meeting of the London District Board of June 1897) had been issued in the previous 12 months and the union had been complaining that they received neither law nor justice from the magistrate.

The article complained about the ill-feeling felt by the "English bakers" towards Jews employed in the same trade. "The usual reckless statements have again been made to the Christian operatives by their leaders and advisors who certainly ought to be better acquainted with their work than they seem to be." It concluded, "What is now required is that we should all be up and doing to remedy through Parliament (the only means) this oppressive law".

John Jenkins of the AUOB had just informed a Brixton audience that "the reason the Jews baked bread on Sunday is not because of supplying members of their own persuasion with bread but ... the great object is that they should supply Christians with bread. It is well known that the Jew supplies five times as much bread to the Christians than to his co-religionist".

"It is news to me," the *Jewish Chronicle* journalist commented, "that the Jew is hungry after the Christian's custom. And has Mr. Jenkins forgotten that there are in the East End of London a large number of Christian bakers who have a large connection with Jewish customers, and who, on Saturdays, have a fine trade with those Jews who would not be classed as froom." [religious][14]

Two weeks later, the *Jewish Chronicle* reported the complaints of bakers from London's West End that they were "suffering from Jewish and other bakers who bake on Sundays. No argument against Sunday work would be complete according to some of our opponents unless the Jews be included. If I remember rightly there are only 3 Jewish bakers in the West End of London. Certainly the number is exceedingly small — not too small however, for our friends to make them bear the sins of the many".

The following month the *Jewish Chronicle* quoted the claim of the *Bakers Times* that Jewish bakers "want by sidewind, as it were, to get the trade of their Christian neighbours", and the *Chronicle*'s correspondent pointed out that, of 40 Jewish baker's shops he passed, only two of them, belonging to one man, were open on

Saturday as well as well as Sunday, while on Sunday between 1 p.m. and 3 p.m. in a Jewish neighbourhood he found 10 Christian bakers open.[15]

On the question of Sunday baking there is no doubt that non-Jewish employers and trade unionists were at one. The *Jewish Chronicle* reported that the London Master Bakers' Association had given more than £69 to the Amalgamated Union towards its expenses in enforcing the law against Sunday baking.[16]

Complaints on the question of Sunday baking persisted into the 20th century. In June 1901 the *Journeymen Bakers Magazine* reminded its readers that the whole issue had been raised 25 years earlier when there were few Jewish bakers. It claimed that over the years Jews had "improved" on Gentiles when it came to sweating and that it was difficult to get convictions against Jews who broke the law on Sunday baking because they took precautions. The magazine also complained that some Jews adopted non-Jewish names.[17] However, the *Jewish Chronicle* reported that when the Jewish Master Bakers' Association had been approached by a deputation from the AUOB on the question of Sunday baking, the association agreed to assist the union in prosecuting any Jewish baker found baking seven days a week.[18]

The case against prosecuting Jewish bakers baking bread on Sundays was neatly put by the well-known Jewish master baker, T. Bonn, who complained "Provided he has kept the Sabbath a Jewish cobbler may make his boots, a Jewish tailor his coat and vests, the Christian publican without fear of prosecution may sell his drinks on the Sunday. But the Jewish baker, even if he has kept his Sabbath, may not bake his bread without the risk of legal proceedings". Bonn appealed against such injustice, although he acknowledged that a seven-day week may well be regarded as a crime.[19] Undoubtedly, some Jewish bakers did employ men to bake on the Jewish Sabbath. A dispute about this dragged on from June or July till at least October or November and was reported at length throughout this period in the *Jewish Chronicle*.

For its part, the International Bakers' Union, in the person of its secretary H. M. Cowen, tried appealing to the ecclesiastical authorities. Of the dozen or so offenders, one, Mr. M. Rosenberg of 42 Philpot St, E1, remained obdurate. The Chief Rabbi urged him to refrain. The Rabbi of Machzike Hadas – the famous orthodox synagogue in Fournier Street, Spitalfields, formerly a church and now a mosque – said that bread baked on the Sabbath day was "as treyf as khazer" (as unclean as pork). The International Bakers' Union tried strike action. None of them succeeded in bringing Mr. Rosenberg to heel.[20]

Meanwhile the AUOB was still actively campaigning to end Sunday baking. The London District Board of the union reported that the sub-committee on Sunday baking had applied for 63 summonses since it was set up.[21] The union journal even reported threats of violence. In July 1901 there was a series of cases at Worship Street Police Court and, at the end of the proceedings on one day, some members of the AUOB were apparently threatened by a number of Jewish men. Fortunately for all concerned Mr. Bonn persuaded the irate Jewish journeymen (who believed these cases were brought for anti-Semitic purposes and, if successful, would threaten their livelihoods) to disperse.[22]

Prosecutions for Sunday baking continued throughout the year and were reported in the trade papers, the union organs, and not least the *Jewish Chronicle*. One magistrate, a Mr. Denham, made a typical comment: "They [the defendants] knew very well they were breaking the law. The truth was that in England they were too easy-going and good-natured. Foreigners were continually breaking the law. The laws of the country must be obeyed. If the defendant wanted to bake bread on Sunday let him go back to Russia, where be could do so without breaking the law".[23] However, while the magistrates displayed a degree of xenophobia in their language, the penalties they imposed were trivial, as those who brought the prosecutions observed bitterly. For example, in the case just mentioned, the penalty was a fine of 10s. plus 5s. costs. Fines of as little as one shilling plus 2s. costs were quite common. It was no wonder that those who broke the law on Sunday baking were not deterred. The name Grodzinski, the best known of Jewish bakers today, crops up repeatedly in the court proceedings for contravening the law on Sunday baking.

Legal actions were expensive. In August 1902 it was estimated that the London Masters Bakers' Association with the AUOB had spent £1000 on initiating proceedings against those who defied the Sunday baking laws.[24] Although Jewish bakers had borne the brunt of the prosecutions, there had also been actions against non-Jewish bakers.

At the end of the year, however, the headline in the *Jewish Chronicle* "Jews and Sunday baking. Prosecutions to cease" must have brought satisfaction to both Jewish master bakers and journeymen. "At a meeting of the London Master Bakers' Protection Society it was decided definitely to suspend the prosecutions hitherto conducted by the Society on account of Sunday baking. Jewish master bakers who closed their shops on Saturday will no longer be annoyed with summonses under an obsolete Act for supplying a general want by baking on Sunday."

The article mentioned the role played by the Jewish master baker Simon Cohen and by the brothers J. and T. Bonn, especially the latter, and the assistance also given by the Jewish Board of Deputies for securing the calling-off of the campaign. The London Master Bakers' Protection Society explained this decision. Defeat was not only because they had not won the sympathy of the magistrates, but they lacked the support of the religious bodies, of the public, and even of the trade. In that year prosecutions had cost them £634 3s. 8d. If they continued they would be bankrupt. The same men were repeatedly prosecuted and the report concludes by mentioning that in the struggle for the rights of Jewish members of the trade "five thousand Christian bakers have been ranged against less than fifty Jewish bakers".[25]

At last the issue of Sunday baking was laid to rest.

Chapter 5. "You Are Our Brothers ... We Wish You Had Not Come"

While the Jewish baking industry was being assailed by critics from without, problems within the industry continued as usual. The International Bakers' Union had protested about a certain baker requiring his men to work for a stretch of 30 hours. Once this had been settled to the union's satisfaction, the secretary of the union was emboldened by this success to announce that a crusade would be launched against the insanitary bakehouses in Whitechapel and Spitalfields.

One master baker was reported in the *Jewish Chronicle* in October 1896 as saying that when he had been a journeyman baker it was not uncommon to work a 36-hour stretch, and that as a master he was earning less than he used to as a journeyman. Indeed so difficult did he find it to make a living that he was selling his business.[1]

Most of the 150 journeymen in employment were unionised. A report at the end of 1896 in the *Jewish Chronicle* claimed that the union, "which has now been in existence for over five years ... numbers 113 members".[2] At this time the journeymen bakers were once again trying to improve their lot by engaging in co-operative production, but their main struggle was being pursued along more traditional lines.

Although the main organ of Jewry, the *Jewish Chronicle*, was generally in tune with what may be called the Jewish establishment, it also dispensed sympathy and advice for the exploited. In its column headed "Jewish Labour Movement", every Jewish worker was enjoined to belong to the union of his trade. "While he remains outside he is helping the manufacturer and the public to live by means of the sweating of the labourers". Indeed the correspondent went further, urging that in every town the members of the different Jewish trade unions should be "affiliated to a Jewish Trades Council, similar to the Trades Councils of London and other towns". The correspondent, ahead of his time, suggested that "earnest thought and careful attention" were required in respect of the organisation of women workers.[3]

The Jewish journeymen bakers did not need much urging, "East London was exceptionally busy last Sunday when a demonstration of journeymen bakers, supported by several unions, passed through the principal thoroughfares of the Jewish quarter. Afterwards a very crowded gathering assembled at the Labour Hall, Cannon Street

Road, where Mr. James Macdonald, Secretary of the London Trades Council, took the chair." After congratulating the bakers on the establishment of their co-operative, he expressed his relief that the Jewish bakers had organised themselves into a union, thereby removing the fear that "the Jewish element would step in and usurp the Gentile workers".[4]

His special condemnation of the baking industry as the only one where men worked such excessively long hours was echoed by Israel Roth, then secretary of the International Bakers' Union, who charged that bakers sometimes worked for 26 hours at a stretch and for as much as 126 hours a week for as little as 2d or twopence-halfpenny an hour. It was to end such sweating the trade union was necessary. Like Macdonald, he accused the sanitary inspectors of turning a blind eye to the conditions in bakeries - underground, dirt everywhere, including in the troughs and in the bread itself.

Another speaker, Mr. Steadman, a member of the London County Council, made the point that whatever the country of origin of workers they needed to fight together against the capitalist class. Indeed for him, not capitalism but divisions within the ranks of the workers, was the great enemy, and the workers united were the masters. The final speaker was Herbert Burrows, famous for his support and encouragement to Jewish workers. They should maintain their Jewish traditions; but as they lived here among English citizens they should become citizens themselves and should play their part in political warfare. Complimenting the Jewish bakery workers on setting an example to English trade unionists in establishing a co-operative bakery, he advocated that bake-houses be placed under the control of the LCC.

In contrast, the *Jewish Chronicle*'s labour correspondent, writing the next month, struck a more sombre note. In his view, the accusation that Jewish workers lacked solidarity was only too often justified, and that when they struck others were ready to step in to do their work for less money, thereby causing those brave enough to go on strike to lose heart.

Some months later the AUOB journal reported another meeting of East End journeymen bakers organised by No. 26 branch, the German branch, at Goulston Street, Aldgate. James Macdonald also addressed this meeting, and reiterated his condemnation of the excessively long hours and insanitary conditions worked in the baking industry. Jacob Jung, the branch secretary, said that though he had done his best to impress upon his fellow Germans the need to assist their English brethren in the trade, unfortunately the German bakers were content to be slaves. For all the criticism of the low union consciousness of Jewish bakery workers, it is clear from this and other evidence that they did not lag behind other, non-Jewish, immigrants in their support of trade unionism. On occasion they were even examples of militancy.

From the columns of the *Jewish Chronicle* at this time, it is clear that the Jewish working class in general was greatly concerned with problems of pay and conditions. However, there was little success in achieving improvements, nor was there much agreement on how to go about it. Little or nothing for the good of the Jewish workingmen had been achieved, claimed the writer on Jewish labour movements, the main cause being "the failure to grasp the elementary principles of trade unions". He castigated the Jewish journeymen — and this was clearly a widely held opinion at the time — for being over-ambitious and in "too great a hurry to become masters themselves". Even when they joined a trade union, the Jewish workmen were content merely to pay the weekly subscription and did not participate actively in the affairs of the union, expecting the secretary to solve all problems. They were advised to study English trade unionism if they wanted to emulate its successes, to note the value of perseverance and not to be indifferent to English methods and to the English language. The writer claimed that it was not unusual that when a Jew addressed a meeting in English rather than Yiddish many showed their disapproval by leaving the room. The point of exposing these defects was to overcome them so that "out of weakness strength may grow".[5]

Perhaps the *Jewish Chronicle* correspondent was not being entirely fair to the new immigrants. While the Jews had strong family and community feeling, the concept of trade unionism was largely unknown to the earliest arrivals. The vast majority of them lacked experience of factory work and of class struggle. Given the anti-Semitism they encountered from British workers, including trade unionists, it required a major effort to get them to appreciate the wisdom of allying themselves with the British trade union movement.

The problems and difficulties of combination were especially great in an occupation like the baking industry, where the numbers in each bakery were so small. It required courage to face up to victimisation, in the knowledge that the small master baker could enlist his family to cope with strikes, and that a pool of unemployed was usually available to step in to replace striking workers. In industries like tailoring it was easier to combine. In factories numbers gave strength and even in small workshops there were more workers to face up to each employer than in bakeries where there may have been only three, four or perhaps half a dozen journeymen.

Despite their small numbers, and their many defeats, the journeymen bakers persisted. They certainly deserved to be congratulated for their efforts to enlist the support of those who had become or were to become famous, not merely nationally, but even internationally, in the labour movement. In September 1897, the International Bakers' Union convened a very well attended meeting in Christchurch Hall, Spitalfields, supported by several Jewish trade unions. This hall was often used, both by Jewish and non-Jewish activists, for protest meetings.

Charlotte Despard, one of the most outstanding figures in the fight for women's suffrage, took the chair. To have won her active support for the struggle to improve the lot of the Jewish journeymen bakers was itself an achievement. Mrs. Despard was among the earliest of the women Poor Law Guardians. She founded clubs for workingmen and boys, and established one of the first child welfare centres in the country (in Nine Elms). She was associated with the pioneer socialists in the Social Democratic Federation. She later stood for Labour in London at the 1918 coupon election, but in the early 20th century was best known as a member of the Women's Social and Political Union and leader of the Women's Freedom League, when it split away from the WSPU. A champion of all progressive causes, Charlotte Despard died in 1939, aged 95.

Mrs. Despard began by reading a letter from Dr. and Mrs. Aveling. The latter, better known as Eleanor Marx, played a key part in the working class movement both in England and internationally. Eleanor Marx had spoken out in the East End of London against the persecution of Jews, and in the latter part of her life proclaimed herself to be a Jewess, affirming that she was the only member of her family to be "drawn to the Jewish people". She showed her sympathy with the Jewish working class when years before she spoke at a meeting called by the United Ladies Tailors Association.[6] Her message of solidarity to the Jewish bakers was sent just a few months before her tragic suicide.

In the letter, sent from Paris, Eleanor Marx and her husband wrote "we feel strongly that a strike unless you can win is not wise. But a strike in which you must win is wisdom. If, as we understand, this is certain - strike and win. We are with you and will do all we can to help you. All good fortune to the International Bakers".

Mrs. Despard said that citizens had a responsibility to ascertain under what conditions the articles they purchased were manufactured. Bread was the staff of life and yet most people were totally ignorant of the manner in which it was produced. Jewish bakers worked from 118 to 126 hours per week for two-pence-farthing to two-pence-halfpenny an hour, in underground bakeries, poorly ventilated and with practically no drainage. A conference of Jewish bakers had decided to call a strike, the timing and other details of which were to be determined at their next meeting. Their union, the International Bakers' Union, had been in existence, she said, for seven years and was affiliated to the London Trades Council, and she called for other unions to support the strikers by refusing to deal at those shops where fair conditions were not observed. It was also necessary to make the great British public aware of the wrongs suffered by the bakers. All had to work shoulder to shoulder if success was to be achieved.

Another famous speaker was Herbert Burrows. He had been the main support of Annie Besant, who had played a leading part in the celebrated match girls' strike of 1888. He had also been one of the most prominent figures in the London gas-workers struggle — victorious without a strike in 1889 — for an eight-hour day. Burrows had always been ready to champion the oppressed Jewish people: in 1895, when the TUC approved a resolution to control immigration at its congress in Cardiff, he had been on the platform alongside Eleanor Marx, Edward Aveling, and the great anarchist Kropotkin at a protest meeting called by 10 London Jewish unions.

Burrows hoped that if the strike did take place it would be successful. Next to the butchers, the bakers, according to a report issued by the LCC, were employed in the most unhealthy occupation in the capital. To win their demands it was essential that the bakers be better organised — of about 130 Jewish journeymen bakers only a half to two-thirds belonged to the Union. He believed that the struggle affected all nationalities and creeds, not merely Jews. It was not just a fight for journeymen bakers. The small bakers needed to fight against the big bakers, the latter against the millers, and all against capitalism.

Jewish immigrants were handicapped, he pointed out, because more of them did not have the vote, because of the arbitrary system of naturalisation, with its £5 fee. It was necessary to ensure that only those prepared to fight on behalf of the disadvantaged should be returned to power. (The difficulties of securing naturalisation, and in particular the high fee, was one that was frequently raised in the Jewish community). Several local Jewish figures also addressed the meeting in Yiddish.

There is no record that this planned strike actually took place. Trade was going through a severe depression. The clothing and the boot and shoe trades were particularly hard hit, and the secretary of the International Bakers' Union, Israel Roth, who had recently also been appointed as secretary of the Cap Makers' Union, said the situation was becoming exceedingly bad.

Despite their own critical difficulties, the Jewish trade unions showed their sense of solidarity by supporting a demonstration on 21 November 1897 in aid of the engineers who were then on strike. It was organised by the Independent Tailors, and the Mantle Makers, other tailoring unions, the Independent Cabinet Makers, the Cigarette Makers, and the International Bakers' Union participated.[7] James Macdonald, secretary of the London Trades Council and the Amalgamated Society of Tailors, paid tribute to the solidarity demonstrated by the Jewish workers in their relations with non-Jewish workers and to the generosity of organised Jewish workers in support of non-Jewish workers who had been locked out. This was echoed at the same meeting by W. J. Pearson, the delegate of the Dockers' Union to the London Trades Council, Compared with non-Jewish trade unions, Pearson observed, Jewish organisations had always been prompt to give their assistance, for example in the 1889 Dock Strike, the 1892 Miners' Strike, and on every eight-hour day demonstration.[8]

The year 1897 had ended sadly for the Jewish bakers. Their cooperative bakery had failed, as had their union's attempt at strike action, and the struggle had to be resumed once again. The AUOB also recognised the need for special action in the Whitechapel area. Even discounting the Jewish element, Whitechapel was different from the rest of London. There were many foreign bakers there, chiefly Germans, who catered for all except Jews. Something other than agitation on the old lines was needed to draw these people away from "low drinking and gambling dens" and to prevent them from becoming the prey of sweaters. One proposal, which the AUOB supported, was the idea of an East London Club for bakers, but this initiative proved abortive.[9]

The next reported attempts to resuscitate the organised Jewish bakers' movement occurred in May 1898. A secretary, I. Jaffe, had been appointed and the offices of the International Bakers' Union were, as previously, at the Red Lion in Black Lion Yard in Whitechapel. A series of meetings — all publicised in the succeeding week in the *Jewish Chronicle* — was organised: on 14 May at the Labour Hall, 167 Cannon Street Road; on 4 June and 17 June at the Mantle Makers' Hall, Whitechapel Road. By August the paper reported that the International Bakers' Union was showing "signs of life" and was "on the move".

An interesting tactic was proposed to end working on the Jewish Sabbath, thereby reducing the total working week, while at the same time answering the campaign of those non-Jewish bakers who opposed Jewish bakeries working on Sundays, on the grounds that many Jewish bakeries also opened on Saturdays. Representatives of the International Bakers' Union and other Jewish unions in the tailoring and mantle makers' industry met with the Sabbath Observance Committee. While the unions were prepared to support the Sabbath observance movement, some of their representatives sought to enlist the Sabbath Observance Committee to back them in their campaign for an eight-hour day, but this the committee refused to entertain "because it was foreign to the object for which they were constituted". Not for the first, nor for the last time, attempts to unite the religious and the trade union wings of Jewry proved fruitless.

The abolition of Sabbath working continued to be discussed frequently. A curious development took place in the autumn of 1899 when "a trade union having for its special object the obtaining of Sabbath rest" was set up, assisted by leading members of the Machzike Hadas,[10] at the Hebrew school *Talmud Torah* in Brick Lane. The other Jewish unions avoided this new venture, considering that it would hinder rather than help their endeavours to obtain better conditions, and it seems not to have survived its initial meeting.

Around the same time, a master baker with several shops, who had previously conceded the bakers' demands for higher wages and the abolition of Sabbath work, tried to break the agreement and restart Saturday work. The committee of the International Bakers' Union appealed to the Chief Rabbi who again said he could do nothing on the matter.[11] The Jewish bakers struck, and on 15 October, assisted by other Jewish organisations, paraded the streets, banners flying, and concluded with an open-air meeting in Philpot Street, E1. For their part, the Jewish Master Bakers' Protection Society (established 6 June 1899) denied that they compelled their men to work on the Sabbath — indeed, they claimed, one of their objects in forming the society was to ensure the abolition of Sabbath working. The Chief Rabbi, Dr. Adler, appealed to nonmembers to join the society and condemned the practice of working on the Sabbath.

At the close of 1899 the *Jewish Chronicle* surveyed the situation within the Jewish unions over that year: "The position of the bakers is still as bad as ever. The International Bakers' Union is weak and cannot do anything for the hardest worked and worst paid of Jewish workmen. Everything has been tried to cause an amelioration — strikes, co-operative bakery etc., but failure has attended all these measures. Owing to abnormally long hours the journeymen bakers have no means of bringing their grievances before the public, and the want of contact, with other workers has, to a great extent, demoralised and discouraged the poor bakers".[12] This was not quite right. As we have seen, the bakery workers did make contact with others. Their failure was more to do with the fact that their membership was scattered in small enterprises, and their employers could replace them either with unskilled scab labour, or by working long hours themselves and calling on their family and relations to work alongside them.

Benjamin Cohen, the secretary of the Jewish Master Bakers' Society, took exception to the *Jewish Chronicle*'s remarks about the evil working conditions of Jewish journeymen bakers. He claimed that the hours and wages of Jewish bakers compared favourably with those of other branches of Jewish labour, that Jewish bakers had constant work, and that their "grievances are brought before the Master Bakers' Union, listened to, and redressed".[13] How far this was from the truth was soon to be seen.

Whatever Benjamin Cohen may have claimed, the grievances of the Jewish bakers were so far from being redressed that on 21 April 1900 the International Bakers' Union brought its 150 members out on strike. They complained that their working day lasted between 18 and 20 hours, and that from Thursday to Friday they worked 30 hours at a stretch in order to keep the Sabbath. They demanded a maximum 12-hour day. The men claimed that they were often forced to work seven days a week for a miserable 12 shillings, and demanded instead a minimum wage of 26 shillings. Although they had recently won an end to Saturday work from most of the masters, this had only been achieved by threatening the masters with proceedings under the Lord's Day Observance Acts. For their part, the employers insisted that their workers could always earn good wages provided they were steady and reliable, but that too many of the men preferred to take casual employment for one or two days a week and to loaf the rest of the week! The employers admitted that hours were somewhat onerous, but claimed that this was a result of the outcry against Sunday trade, which meant that they had to close their business two days a week on both the Jewish and Christian Sabbath.[14]

On the following day, Sunday 22 April, a demonstration was held in support of the strikers, marching through the main streets of the East End. The unions of the Jewish Cabinet Makers, Cap Makers and Tailors supported the bakers, as did the AUOB. In the evening a crowded meeting was held at the "York Minster" in Philpot Street, where a collection was held to raise funds for the strikers, whose union had only £3 in the funds and could not give them any strike pay. Five days later, the *Jewish Chronicle* reported that four master bakers had already accepted the men's terms.[15] Discussions between the masters and the men were held, but broke down on certain points, for example, on the men's demand to have a walking delegate admitted to any place where union men were employed. Further demonstrations and open-air meetings were held and soon 12 masters had agreed to the men's terms.

On Saturday 12 May, while the Jewish bakers' strike was still underway, the AUOB held a protest demonstration that evening against the employers' failure to adhere to their agreement to a 10-hour day and a minimum rate of pay. A large contingent from the International Bakers' Union headed by their banner joined the non-Jewish bakers in a huge procession winding its way through the East End of London. In Fieldgate Street, as the demonstration passed by a Jewish master baker's shop — probably the first bakery opened in 1888 by Grodzinski — the band leading the way struck up the Dead March from Saul. The bakery proprietor, probably alarmed by the implication of the music, complained to the police who ordered the musicians to stop playing the march. The police were ignored, however, and at least a dozen times when passing bakers' shops which flouted union terms, the Dead March was played. The Poplar Branch of the AUOB made a point of congratulating the organized Jewish bakers on their "bold and gallant stand".[16]

In June 1900 the *Jewish Chronicle* pointed to the increasing activity of the Jewish unions and to the continuing struggle of the Jewish bakers. Although they had persuaded 16 masters to accept their terms, 68 men were still on strike. The paper's labour correspondent referred to the feeling "among the more thoughtful sections of the Jewish unions" that steps needed to be taken to safeguard the funds of their organisations. The correspondent applauded Herbert Burrows' suggestion that the time was ripe to create a Jewish Trades and Labour Council.

There had already been sporadic attempts unite the Jewish trade union movement. The most important had taken place under socialist sponsorship, when an East London Federation of Labour Unions was inaugurated at a mass meeting in the Great Assembly Hall, Mile End Road, on 28 December 1889. Tom Mann, Ben Tillett and an array of Yiddish orators addressed the meeting. The federation was not Jewish in name, but all of its constituent bodies were Jewish, although at that time the bakers were not among them. However, it came to nothing.[17] Moreover, for all Tillett's encouragement, even his feelings were not unreservedly friendly. Just before the end of the century he is reported to have said of the Jewish trade unionists: "Yes, you are our brothers and we will do our duty by you, but we wish you had not come".[18]

Chapter 6. The New Century

The affairs of the Jewish bakers were next in the news in April 1901, when the *Jewish Chronicle* reported that official representatives of the various Jewish unions were investigating the affairs of the International Bakers' Union. Nine months previously, the union had received considerable contributions to its strike fund, but no account had been presented either to the union members or to the public at large. There were fears that the very existence of the union was in peril, especially as the Registrar of Friendly Societies had threatened the officials of the union with imprisonment if they did not pay the fine imposed for neglect to make the last annual return.[1]

The Jewish bakers' problems were not unique. The London Tailors' Union, for example, was similarly affected. Outside the capital, on the other hand, Jewish trade unions were flourishing. In Leeds the Amalgamated Jewish Tailors, Pressers, and Machinists, which practically controlled the whole of the tailoring trade in Leeds, had a membership of about 2000, possessed its own clubroom, and had capital of about £800. There was obviously much to be learned from this, the most successful Jewish trade union in the United Kingdom. Incidentally, there was the International Tailoress' Union, "the only Jewish women's trade society in England, if not in the world",[2] which was also based in Leeds. The *Jewish Chronicle* labour correspondent suggested that the Jewish unions in the provinces enjoyed greater success because they were more persevering, less quarrelsome, and more fraternally inclined than were the London Jewish unions.

The *Jewish Chronicle*'s survey of the Jewish trade union movement in early 1902 noted a lull in the Jewish labour world, but conceded that a relaxation of trade union effort in times of depression is not unusual. The past year had been "prolific of new organisations", but a few unions formed during the year had succumbed to adverse circumstances owing to precipitate strikes. Eleven new unions had come into existence - seven in the clothing trade alone — and 13 old unions had maintained their *status quo*, but three or four societies were in a precarious position. "Of these the bakers and the Jewish National Tailors' Union are a sad example".

1901 had been "a year of revolt" in Jewish labour affairs. No fewer than 30 societies had "taken part in the general movement for bringing about a higher standard of life", but "the grand effort to establish a central organisation connecting all the various societies for defensive and offensive purposes had received the support of but a few unions". Many of the leading lights of the Jewish labour movement had moved on to America, which had undoubtedly weakened the unions in England. However, the article continued, "though 1901 closed with many disappointments, 1902, though somewhat quiescent, opens with renewed hope and bright prospects".[3]

Yet reports of inertia, disorganisation, the lack of experienced leadership and the need for the amalgamation of trade unions, for example in tailoring, continued to appear in the *Jewish Chronicle* throughout the year. Herbert Burrows tried constantly to remedy this situation. He spoke frequently at meetings, not only to promote trade unionism among the Jewish working-class, but also against the continuing anti-alien movement. The quiescence of the Jewish bakers' union reflected the demoralisation throughout the Jewish labour movement. The Jewish journeymen bakers were largely inactive for the first nine months of 1902.

This apathy was commented on in the *Jewish Chronicle*. "Just over a year ago the International Bakers' Union reached its lowest watermark owing to the strike in which it was conquered by Mr. Rosenberg and has not been heard of during the whole year". There were signs that they were, perhaps for the fourth or fifth time, anxious to reorganise themselves. Whether they had profited from their experience remained to be seen. They were proposing to change the name of the union from the International Bakers' Union to the Jewish National Bakers' Union in the hope, perhaps, that this change of name would bring better luck![4]

In 1903, the affairs of the Jewish bakers, and the persistent grievances of those who worked for the Jewish master bakers, received further publicity. In an article titled "Bakers' Discontent" the *Jewish Chronicle* labour correspondent highlighted the differences between the native English workers and the Jewish workers. The grievances of English workers, he argued (not entirely correctly if we remember the strikes of the Match Girls and the Dockers), would be articulated by a pre-existing, more or less well-organised body. With the Jewish workers, the complaints themselves were used as the means of forming the organisation. As the grievances of the Jewish workers, though genuine, were not felt with equal conviction by all in the trade, solid organisation seldom or never resulted. "In spite of all this, a course of hasty or ill-advised action, commenced in a half-hearted manner without funds, or even the support of those in the trade, is usually resorted to, ending in failure". The writer continued that this was "the history of every

Jewish union in London, the history of complaints and misdirected efforts".

He condemned the way that the Jewish journeymen bakers had thrown away opportunities because of their apathy and the mismanagement of their leaders, which had landed them in trouble and disgrace more than once. Within the past eight years co-operative production and distribution had started several times, but through their own faults had ended in failure. On each occasion a large Jewish public had been in sympathy with their aims, and had supported them by showing a preference for their products. By the exercise of foresight, ability and determination they could have controlled the trade. "Incapacity, jealousy and selfish motives had shattered their hopes and prevented them from holding their masters at bay". The men's leaders then had no other recourse than "ill-conceived and ill-managed strikes". There was a lack of solidarity and of funds despite the generosity of the public to whom they appealed, and so the strikes collapsed. The unions refused to publish their accounts, resulting "in the parading of the union affairs before the magistrate, throwing some discredit on the Jewish bakers and their methods of organisation".

The correspondent accused both the leaders and the rank and file of not knowing their own minds, of changes in their objectives, of unpreparedness, lack of organisation, and a failure to profit by a study of their past history. Some of these criticisms were perhaps sweeping or unjust. The correspondent failed to recognise the bakers' enormous difficulties given the way their industry was organised — small bakeries where it was not unduly difficult to replace "troublemakers", either from a pool of unemployed who could be easily trained, or at least temporarily from the employer's own family. He showed little appreciation of the fact that the bakers had little tradition of trade union struggle to call upon. Nonetheless, he was surely right to castigate their present demands, which took "the ridiculous form of a request addressed to the Chief Rabbi to order sermons to be preached on their behalf". In view of the Chief Rabbi's stance on labour disputes, it is difficult to disagree with the correspondent's assessment and his remark that "such tactics are characterised as bearing the impress of sheer stupidity and are not regarded seriously by labour men". Instead of invoking the aid of influential persons, he urged organisation as the best form of self-help and the first step towards improvement in the conditions of labour.[5]

The following week, the *Jewish Chronicle* returned to the problem of proper financial accountability. "The want of proper accounts in connection with Jewish trade unionists has always acted as a deterrent upon a large number of workers and still remains an unsolved problem. To this may in no small degree be attributed their aloofness from the organisations". The paper also mentioned that the Jewish master bakers of East London had agreed to meet their workers' representatives in conference on the following Monday to discuss hours and wages. The employers were even prepared to allow Herbert Burrows to preside over the conference, which was evidence of the respect he enjoyed.

Religious differences did not prevent Jewish trade unions from acting jointly and displaying solidarity with other fellow trade unionists. On Sunday 25 January 1903, for example, the Jewish Trade Union Committee convened a meeting at the Independent Cabinet Makers' hall at 4 Wilkes Street, Spitalfields, attended by both non-Jews and Jews, with delegates from 10 East End Societies.[5] This committee had been formed by the United Cardboard Box Makers to protest against the forced starvation of the women and children of the Bethesda Quarry Miners, locked out by Lord Penrhyn, and to enlist practical sympathy and support on their behalf. Herbert Burrows presided, and speakers included Israel Roth, secretary of Jewish Bakers' Union, and S. Ellstein, then the leader of the tailors, who later took over as Jewish Bakers' Union secretary. In addition to speaking in support of the Welsh mining community, Ellstein rebutted the oft-repeated charge that workers accepted the lowest wages, insisting that while their wages were not as high as they should be, they were comparable with, if not better than, those of non-Jewish English workers.

On the next day Herbert Burrows presided, yet again, at a conference of Jewish master bakers and their employees at the King's Hall in Commercial Road, (later well known as a venue for the presentation of plays performed in Yiddish). Israel Roth in his speech said men were working anything from 16 to over 20 hours a day. As for pay, foremen were paid fourpence-halfpenny an hour, second hands twopence-three farthings an hour, and third hands twopence-farthing an hour. The Jewish master bakers, who imposed these conditions, often held responsible positions in the synagogue. This presumably prompted Roth to write to the Chief Rabbi on 31 December 1902, complaining of "the slavery under which Jewish bakers had to work" and asking him to instruct all the

London Jewish Ministers under his supervision to preach a sermon against such a state of things.

The *Jewish Chronicle* thought such a request "stupid", and the Chief Rabbi himself was not prepared to put just one side of the case. More surprisingly, he also stated that he "could not see what good could arise from preaching on the subject" — a remarkable lack of faith in the efficacy of sermons! He was, however, prepared to give some practical aid. "If you will attend at the Beth Hamedrash [House of Study of Synagogue] I will see whether some conference could be arranged between the East London Bakers Union and the employers".

At the King's Hall conference, Israel Roth proposed that men's hours of labour should not exceed 12 daily and 72 a week. There should be no overtime; foremen's wages should be £2 a week; second hands' wages 32s.; third hands' 25s.; fourth hands' 21s., and finally, the union should be recognised. In the ensuing discussion some of the masters denied emphatically that hours were that long, and claimed that wages exceeded the union's own demands. After some discussion Mr. Levy, on behalf of the masters present, expressed readiness to recognise the men's union and to work with it to improve conditions of labour. A joint committee of employers and men was appointed to draw up an equitable scheme for submission to a future conference.

On 8 February 1903, the East London Social Democratic Federation held a crowded meeting at the Wonderland, a popular centre for boxing events on Whitechapel Road. It was addressed by Mr. Griffin, organiser of the London AUOB. He spoke out against sweated labour, and demanded the enforcement of the Factory and Public Health Act. He spoke of his own part in helping to organise the Jewish bakers and claimed that the joint conference would lead to an improvement in working conditions for the Jewish bakers.

S. Ellstein seconded Mr. Griffin's resolution and deplored the lack of organisation among Jewish workers, and the London organiser of the SDF attacked the press for trying to blame the trade depression on the Jews.[6]

On 16 February 1903 the conference of masters and men was resumed at the King's Hall, and Israel Roth presented a statement drawn up by the joint committee appointed three weeks previously. It had been agreed that the men should assist the Masters' Association, while the masters in turn undertook to employ only union men and to accept the union label. An overtime rate of 9d an hour had been agreed, any future differences were to be settled by arbitration, and Sabbath work was to cease. Some of the masters objected to accepting the union label unless theirs could also be used. The other decisions of the joint committee were confirmed, while the union label question was referred back.

However bad things were for Jews in London, the situation was much worse for Jews in the Russian Empire and Eastern Europe. Following the pogrom in Kishinev during Passover 1903, in which 49 Jews were killed and hundreds fled, the Jewish Bakers' Union took part in protests "against the 20th century barbarities of Russian civilisation". These protests were initiated by the Independent Cabinet Makers, which convened a conference of delegates from trade and labour societies and invited English labour and kindred organisations to join a demonstration on 21 June 1903 against the Kishinev massacres. Thousands marched from Mile End to Hyde Park, where 25,000 supporters listened to speeches, from three platforms, in English, Yiddish, Polish and Russian.

Around the same time, the affair of the "bagel bakers" received considerable coverage in the Jewish press. The word bagel (or "beigel") is derived from the German "Beugel", "a round loaf of bread". These "ring rolls," doughnut shaped, are simmered in boiling hot water before baking, then glazed with egg-white. The bagel bakers were among the most downtrodden sections of the Jewish proletariat. As the *Jewish Chronicle* put it, the bagel bakers were "useful members of society", but the pleasure their handiwork daily afforded was hardly given fair recognition. The bagel makers were sweated even more than the lowliest journeymen bakers. They worked between 18—20 hours a day for a miserable pittance of something between 1s. 9d and 2s. 6d.[7]

The savage extent of their exploitation was raised by Messrs. Solomons and Diamonston, representatives of the tailors, at the weekly meeting of the Jewish Organisation Committee. The bagel men had decided they would rather starve than continue to tolerate their dreadful conditions, and had come out on strike. Starve they obviously would without financial help, for up to then they had been unorganised, and had no funds. Solomons and Diamonston urged that the committee give them its active support. Some delegates strongly objected to supporting non-union workmen, whose past actions might well have harmed the interests of the organised bakers. By assisting the unorganised, they argued, the committee was rewarding the negligence and inactivity of those who persistently stood aloof, who refused to bear the expense of organisation but were ready to ask for practical sympathy and lay claim to the generosity of others. However, the majority disagreed. The committee had been formed with the object of organising the workers, and they owed a duty to these suffering people. This was a more reasonable line to pursue than turning the cold shoulder. An investigating committee was appointed to act jointly with the Jewish Bakers' Union, and as a result the bagel bakers also joined the union.

On 11 September 1903, the General Jewish Workers Organisation Committee organised a well attended gathering at Christchurch Hall, Hanbury Street — one of the most popular meeting places for East London workers — to draw attention to the need for East End Jewish workers to organise.[8] The speakers included Rudolf Rocker, the Anarchist leader and champion of the Jewish workers — a non-Jew who had learned to speak and write Yiddish — and Griffin, a leading figure in the AUOB. They stressed the need for Jew and non-Jew to unite against those who sweated them and were sufficiently understanding to recognise (in a way that the *Jewish Chronicle* labour correspondent often could not) that "it was impossible to expect that the Jewish workers, escaping from the lands of persecution and oppression, would suddenly develop trade union organisation on a scale comparable to the English trade unions, whose strong position had been built up during many years of comparative freedom".

One of the many problems of trade union organisation among Jewish workers was that they could not afford permanent offices or full-time organisers. Their meeting places — pubs were popular — frequently changed, and one organiser often served for two or more trade unions. In October 1903, for example, it was reported that S. Ellstein had recently given up his position as organiser of the London Mantle Makers but "in addition to his secretarial duties in connection with the Cigarette Makers' Union, he has also undertaken to serve the Military Tailors' Union and the Jewish Bakers' Union".[9] Ellstein's appointment was a cause for widespread optimism. He had done much to boost the membership of the Cigarette Makers' Union, and was to become an important figure in the affairs of the Jewish journeymen bakers in London. The *Jewish Chronicle*'s labour correspondent certainly expected that this would mean brighter prospects for the union. He also reported that the East London Bakers' Union (the former name "International Bakers' Union" had fallen into disuse) had registered a label to be affixed to loaves baked with union labour. The plan was to ask the masters to adopt it and to urge the public to buy only bread bearing this label.[10]

By November 1903 the joint committee of masters and journeyman bakers had broken down. It appeared that only one master was willing to serve on it, and that the masters as a whole rejected any changes in the *status quo*. The union could see no purpose in its continued existence. Jewish workers generally felt that the East London Bakers' Union had tried its best to negotiate with the masters, but now the only practical way forward was open agitation.

At a public meeting organised by the East London Bakers in December 1903, Ellstein hammered home the distressing conditions his members endured, and named the employers who compelled their employees to work on the Sabbath. However, he conceded that the union was weak because "there were about 200 Jewish journeymen bakers, but a good many had become utterly insensible to their sufferings and stood aloof from the union which, if well organized, would command the respect of the employers". The two other main speakers were non-Jewish. Harry Quelch, of the Social Democratic Federation and editor of its weekly, *Justice*, expressed his total support for the Jewish journeymen bakers, but complained that so many of them "were always dreaming of becoming master men", when they should be organising themselves against the masters. In any event the opportunities of becoming master bakers were fewer and fewer each year. If there was any anti-Semitic feeling in the country, this "was not made on the grounds of nationality or race, but on the ground of their coming here to do the Englishmen's work at lower wages. It was incumbent on the bakers not only to organize, but the Jewish public generally to give the bakers every assistance in their power".[11]

Chapter 7. 1904: A Momentous Year

Reynolds News was one of the first papers to report Jewish workers' determination to defend and improve their standards in 1904. An article headed "industrial Israelites" reported that a Jewish co-operative and distributive society had been established in the East End of London. One hundred Jewish workers had already taken out £1 shares. "In addition to supplying the members with goods at current market prices, evening classes will be opened and lectures given, and everything that will tend to elevate and educate the masses". The failure of previous attempts to start co-operative productive societies in the tailoring, cabinet making, and baking trades was ascribed to "jealousies among its members and all of them wanting to be managers".[1]

Reynolds News gave a lot of coverage to labour affairs, including Jewish labour affairs. But while it claimed to champion the fight for justice, it displayed an ambivalent attitude towards Jews. For example, one *Reynolds News* editorial proclaimed "Today the Jews govern the world" ... "they have captured the press".[2] It published crude cartoons[3], as well as some blatantly anti-Semitic "jokes", such as: "Why you putting the boy in the safe Israel?" — "He's swallowed a diamond". At the same time, the paper claimed that it "always fought against unreasoning prejudice". Certainly it was the only national newspaper that reported that the East End Jewish bakers were threatening to strike that coming April. It set out their demands, which had been announced at the Black Bull Public House, Old Montague Street, and commented that the time chosen for striking was "opportune"... "as for fully six days from next Tuesday no bread will be baked owing to the Jewish Passover". *Reynolds News* reminded its readers that "the grievances of the Jewish bakers were recorded in these columns when no other paper would take up their cause".[4]

The East London Bakers' Union required that its demands be met by 3 April, otherwise it would strike. The *Jewish Chronicle* commented, "a strike of Jewish bakers with all the sad consequences it had in store for the parties concerned will be nothing new in the East End. The time has indeed been well chosen. For the absence of leavened bread at the termination of the Passover holidays, at a time when hungry crowds most eagerly await it, is calculated to give the men the best advertisement and to advance their cause".[5] However much the Jewish public might look forward to Passover with matzos [unleavened bread] replacing bread, after eight days of a diet of matzos, many yearned for the usual diet of rye bread, chollahs, bagels and platzels.

The union's main demands were: a trade union label to be placed on every loaf (masters could use their own label in addition); a maximum 12-hour day; no overtime except for two hours on Thursday (so that there could be enough bread for both Friday and the Sabbath, when bakeries were closed) such overtime to be paid at the rate of time-and-a-half; a minimum wage of 26s a week; no master baker to be allowed to work in his own bakehouse, and one class of worker not to do the work of another class; only members of the East London Bakers' Union to be employed; and delegates of the union to have access to the bakehouses for trade union purposes.

The union held a demonstration on Sunday 10 April to launch the strike. There were so many supporters that extra police were on duty, especially to prevent interference with baker's shops. The large crowd was addressed mainly by Yiddish and German speakers. A reporter from the *Daily Express* present obviously felt that he was being transported into another world. In his report he emphasised repeatedly the "strangeness" of the "picturesque procession", which contained in its mile and a half length "a bevy of dark-eyed Jewish tailoresses bearing banners inscribed with Jewish characters ...a long fantastic crowd of pale aliens singing something to the air of the great French hymn in strong guttural staccato". He also made play of the onlookers, many of whom were to join the march, as including "Hebrew patriarchs with flowing beards, women in gaudy sky blue and red ...squat men, suffering victims of European oppression" and to the confusion of tongues. However novel the scene was to him, the great novelty for the "surging crowds of Russian, German, Polish, Balkan and other Jews" occurred, he thought, when the onlookers were actually addressed in English by one of the supporting speakers.[6] Perhaps the most surprising thing is that a national newspaper — the item appeared on the front page of the *Express* — bothered to report a localised trade dispute.

The *Bakers Record* remarked, "The fact that they were able to march through the streets, protected by the police, has filled some of them with amazement". This was hardly surprising, considering that in their native countries they were grateful to be allowed to live without molestation! The report continued: "Those who know the East End, say that their action is only typical of what is going on among all the Jewish workers, who in the future will not be content to work for any wages and under any conditions that may be offered them". The reaction of the *Bakers Record* reporter, who visited the strikers' headquarters at Wilkes Street on the Tuesday afternoon after the march, was even more revealing: "They looked a very respectable body of men, entirely different to the preconceived notion of the pauper alien — helpless, hopeless, ragged and dirty. Their conduct so far has been perfectly orderly. Indeed they seem scarcely to understand yet that their action has not brought them within the reach of the law".[7]

Under the heading "Aliens' successful revolt", *Reynolds News* expressed its views forthrightly. It observed that the 300 or so Jewish bakers were by no means the servile "dirty, pauper aliens" that a lot of people imagined. Although it considered the Jewish union's demands to be modest, they were nevertheless more than most "freedom loving British bakers" got and more than they were prepared to demand. It cited this fact against the tremendous agitation then underway against alien immigration which asserted that "foreign labourers who come to our shores are willing to work long hours for starvation wages and to do anything to under-sell British labour". *Reynolds News* commented that the strike, "though in itself a small affair throws much light on the question of alien immigration. This strike is an indication of the agitation and constant organisation which is always going on among other alien workers, especially the Jews in the East End, who, we are convinced, are not content to work ... for any wage and under any condition that may be offered".[8]

Rudolf Rocker, editor of the Yiddish-language anarchist paper *Arbeter Fraynd*, described the demonstration as "a manifestation of solidarity and fraternity such as I have never seen". Everywhere there was talk only of the bakers' strike, he wrote. Carried away by enthusiasm, the sub-heading of his article was, prematurely, "the beginning of victory".[9] Subsequent issues of the *Arbeter Fraynd* published long lists of donations, demonstrating the support for the strikers. Small as these contributions may now seem, ranging from 1d upwards, they represent a sacrifice for the poverty-stricken inhabitants of the East End.[10]

There were some immediate successes. Interviewed in the *Daily Express* for its report of the demonstration, union secretary Ellstein claimed that 48 Jewish master bakers were affected by the strike, and that five of the largest masters, employing nearly one third of the striking journeymen, had agreed to the men's terms that very day. After initial resistance the journeymen at these five big employers agreed to return to work from the Wednesday — they had wanted to stay out until all the employers gave way.

On the first Monday bread had to be obtained either from Christian bakers or from the few Jewish bakers able to bake with assistance from their relatives. "A curious feature" was that the Christian bakers did not advance the price, while the Jewish bakers put up the price from fivepence-halfpenny to 7d a quartern.[11] By Wednesday, 13 April, the strike appeared to have been all but won. At 11 of the 48 bakehouses concerned — who employed the majority — the men returned with the assurance that all their demands would be granted. The other employers were small firms, employing perhaps one journeyman apiece. On the Wednesday evening when the first batches came out hot from the ovens there was a rush for the "union" bread.

The next week, however, the *Jewish World* noted that some 30 to 40 of the smaller employers still stubbornly refused to give way. It reported a great demonstration of Jews of all nationalities on the previous Sunday. "With a huge loaf decked with many coloured streamers borne aloft on a platform", they marched through miles of streets and called on their supporters "not only to buy union labelled bread exclusively, but also to leave off buying your tea, butter, eggs, and other provisions at shops which sell bread baked in non-union bakehouses".[12]

At the end of April the *Jewish Chronicle* dealt extensively with the dispute. It reported that thousands had joined the demonstration on the Sunday after the strike was announced, although the number of strikers did not exceed 300. After the march "one of the largest meetings ever [was] held at Bucks Row, Whitechapel". The paper asserted that the strike was practically over, that only a few insignificant master bakers were holding out and concluded: "This comparatively quick and easy victory is calculated to give an impetus to trade union agitation".[13]

But all was not over! Indeed it became clear that the small masters were determined not to give way to strikers. As the *Bakers Record* reported, "Those few master bakers who have signed the union conditions have kept them honourably, but the remaining 30 masters have reduced the price of bread to 4d per quartern in order to draw off the custom of those who paid the union wages and observed the conditions. This has been a success, as the Jewish foreign women will buy in the cheapest market irrespective of whether the bread is baked under union conditions" — as if Jewish women were any different from their fellow non-Jews in this respect! This had led the masters from union shops to appeal to the union "for help in spreading the label, otherwise they would have to revert to the old conditions against their will".[14]

The strike was still dragging on in May. The *Jewish Chronicle* published another detailed examination of the dispute, headed "The Bakers' Stand". "There is general agreement among labour men that defeat would overcast with gloom the labour organizations and would be taken as a defeat of Jewish labour as a whole. Hence all the active spirits have put aside their theoretic differences and are concentrating their efforts to lead the bakers to certain victory. It is interesting that they do not rely on mere agitation or appeal to the generosity of the public, but they have attacked the position from a business standpoint determined to give the idea of self-help practical application. For preparations are well ahead to start the strikers in work on a co-operative basis ...[the] leaders are warranted in looking forward to the future with much confidence".[15]

Signed articles by Ellstein, the bakers' leader, appeared weekly between 29 April 1904 and 10 June 1904 in the *Arbeter Fraynd* indicating the progress of the strike and appealing for continued support. While the calls for financial assistance were becoming more strident – understandably, as the union was also involved in a case before the High Court – until the beginning of June Ellstein seemed in no doubt that the strike would end in victory. He referred with satisfaction to the disunity of the masters, which coupled with the boycott of their shops, forced some of the most obstinate and "farbissener" [hard line] of the employers to settle with the Union. Indeed a number who had previously agreed to accept the union's demands and had then retracted were again compelled to concede and even to pay a fine of two guineas and to dismiss scabs before the union would permit them to resume normal baking. With ruin staring them in the face, surrender was the only way out for the masters.[16]

As for the union's plans to set up a baking co-operative, a writer in the *Jewish Chronicle* on 20 May 1904 stressed the need for enthusiasm, proper management, and a sufficiency of working capital. Although all these seemed to be present there were doubts about the existence of real co-operative spirit, self-restraint and the absence of petty jealousies. The *Arbeter Fraynd*, on the other hand, had no such qualms. On 20 May it reported that the bakehouse and its offices were to be at 186 Cable Street. Other unions had pledged solidarity — the Jewish tailors had offered aprons and the Jewish cap-makers would donate caps. The writer optimistically forecast that further co-operatives would be opened. The master bakers were obviously worried about the dangers of a successful co-operative enterprise, but it would seem that the chief obstacle to resuming meaningful negotiations was their unwillingness to adopt the trade union label — a central demand of the union.

This opposition to the use of the label was expressed in a letter to the *Jewish Chronicle* from a master baker, who also blamed the strike on "paid agitators". A meeting was held at the home of a master baker, Mr. Rosenberg of 54 High Street, Whitechapel, to co-ordinate the masters' position. Simon Cohen, the oldest Jewish baker, was invited along to advise on the crisis. His suggestions included that "one shilling shall be given from each sack of flour to form a fund from which assistance could be granted to the small bakers to obtain a living ... by this means the trade would go on in its usual way".[17]

By early June, there was a desperate note of urgency in an appeal by Ellstein, aimed especially at readers of workers' and progressive newspapers. He reminded his readers in the *Arbeter Fraynd* that the strike had been going for eight weeks, emphasised that this was a pioneering action in the fight to secure Jewish trade union rights, and begged for aid: "Will you stand by and see us have to give up the struggle because we don't have the funds to continue the battle with the masters and the courts"?[18] Two weeks later, Ellstein wrote to the *Jewish Chronicle*, repudiating the charge that the strike was the work of paid agitators. He insisted that neither he nor anyone else had ever "made a living out of the Bakers Union", and stressed the modesty of the men's demands: "the maximum number of hours we ask from the masters is 14 above what the English baker now works". The demand for the trade union label was "in order that we and the public may know that the agreed conditions of labour are observed".[19]

The East London Bakers' Union received material support not only from Jewish trade unions in London and the provinces, notably Leeds and Manchester, but also from the AUOB. The *Journeymen Bakers Magazine* for July 1904 reported that the London District AUOB Branch "Executive had granted £5 to the Jewish bakers and had also made them a loan of £50, which was received with satisfaction".[20]

In the early days of the strike the mood of the journeyman bakers had been euphoric, while the mood of the masters was one of alarm. However, towards the end of June "the termination of the strike on the part of the Union [was] officially announced".[21] How had the strike gone from seemingly certain success to sudden collapse? The national union, the AUOB, seemed to have no doubts. Reporting that the £50 loan to the Jewish Bakers had been repaid, it announced that the strike had been "closed — about 60 of the men having to go back to work under the best conditions they could obtain, chiefly through English and German non-unionists having black-legged the shops".[22] In other words the failure did not stem from a lack of solidarity or enthusiasm on the part of the Jewish bakers. However, divisions between the Jewish political organisations supporting the strikers did not help. Not for the first time proponents of rival political ideologies castigated each other for treachery and accused each other of responsibility for the strikers' defeat.

Remarkably, the anarchist *Arbeter Fraynd* did not print a word about the strike between 17 June and 1 July 1904. Nor did it clearly report the strike's sudden collapse, nor the reasons for its failure. However, it did launch a bitter assault[23] on "the anonymous smears and lies" published in the *Naye Tsayt*, the organ of the East London [Jewish] Social Democrats.[24] In a leading article headed "Finale of the Bakers' Strike" *Naye Tsayt* ascribed its disastrous outcome, after there was every prospect of victory, to the "incapable light-headed strike committee composed mostly of anarchists", who had refused to allow those masters who were about to concede to cut the price of their bread so that they could compete with those who had already surrendered. The anarchists had also led the bakers into the "swamp" of the co-operative bakery. *Naye Tsayt* denounced the "wild fancies" and "the feverish queries" of the anarchists for whom "the workers' movement is a kind of theatre", and who were "trying to drag the strike on till the messiah comes, and were rehearsing social revolution". For native trade unionists, *Naye Tsayt* argued, the strike weapon was a last resort; it was then "takke" [indeed truly] a strike, well organised, financially well-based, and united. The Jewish workers, in contrast, rushed into strikes without sufficient money or stable organization, and were only too ready to engage in "heymishe" [home made, naive] experiments. Ellstein himself had stated that "it is not the bakers who are striking, but they are being struck for" — presumably others were more enthusiastic for the strike than the strikers themselves.

There is no doubt that the anarchists were the staunchest and most consistent backers of the strike, helped raise substantial sums for it (Rocker himself went to the provinces to appeal for money, especially among the Jewish trade unions), and provided most of the speakers for the strikers. They may have been over-optimistic and unable to recognise the difficulties that confronted inexperienced and at times apathetic strikers. However, they had not been the only ones to imagine, when things first went well, that victory was within the bakers' grasp, and that such a victory would be an example and an inspiration to the rest of the Jewish working class movement in England.

The *Jewish Chronicle's* labour correspondent published a critical study of the conduct of the strike, although here he was being wise after the event. Less than two months previously he had been writing that the journeymen bakers' leaders could reasonably look forward with confidence to the future. [25] In his analysis, one factor which probably contributed to defeat was the Court of Appeal's dismissal of the union's appeal in the case of East London Bakers' Union v. Goldstein, discussed below. The blow to morale and the financial burden suffered by the union arising out of this case undermined the spirit of the striking unionists. The strikers had hoped for a speedy victory, for they could not afford a prolonged strike. Early successes seemed to give grounds for optimism, but the obduracy of the small masters caused the strike to drag on. Although the public gave generously, the union still had to find funds to support about 50 men every week. The *Jewish Chronicle* correspondent blamed the strike committee for declaring a strike without adequate financial and moral preparation. Moreover, he accused it of a series of blunders from the inception of the struggle, including an inability to negotiate. He claimed that the masters who had stood out were on the point of yielding, but in order to win back lost customers, they would have had to reduce the price of bread; but the men's committee refused to sanction this, insisting that they agree to maintain market prices. In this way, he charged, the committee threw away a chance of a settlement "favourable to the prestige and position of the Union".

The labour correspondent argued that the decision to establish a co-operative bakery represented a more serious blunder, in that the strike committee had thereby, "diverted into other channels the financial support upon which the strike depended for its successful termination". In fact, the co-operative bakery had only been able to give employment to half-a-dozen men. Then, after a members' meeting, the East London Bakers' Union had decided to take no further part in the co-operative bakery, a decision the writer attacked as "feverish haste to wreck a movement upon which much labour and energy has been expended", which illustrated "the characteristic impatience of the Jewish workers". A month later the committee in charge of the co-operative bakery decided to suspend operations, and the *Jewish Chronicle* wrote that the "untimely end of the enterprise" was even more disappointing than the abandonment of the bakers' strike. All the hopes that the co-operative would teach the workers self-help and might pressurise the masters into conceding the workers' demands had been dashed. With the superior quality of the co-operative bread, demand had exceeded supply, and the efficiency of the organisation had been sound under the management of J. Rosen, former secretary of the Mantle Makers' Union. However, his resignation, along with a lack of mutual confidence between those involved in the enterprise had hastened its demise.[26] Similarly, given the odds against it, it was not surprising that the strike failed, despite the enthusiasm it engendered and despite the wide experience of its leader, Ellstein.

At the time the strike collapsed in June, the East London Bakers' Union called a meeting at the Wonderland to review the position.[27] The union leadership was not immediately downcast or convinced that the strike had been altogether a failure. The union expressed its determination to continue its agitation for the trade union label. It drew attention to those who had won better conditions in the strike, and pledged itself to defend and improve their lot. Finally, it urged the journeymen bakers to prepare financially and morally to fight for more in the future. However, blow after blow was raining down upon the union. It proved unable to follow through the gains made at the beginning of the strike. The Court of Appeal found against the union in June. The co-operative bakery failed. The complete abandonment of the strike was announced,[28] and by January 1905 the union itself had been formally dissolved.[29]

The collapse of the strike represented a defeat not merely for the bakers but for the whole Jewish trade union movement. At the end of 1904, J. Rosen, the former manager of the Jewish co-operative bakery, wrote in the *Jewish Chronicle*, castigating the Jewish workers for their negligence and unwillingness to part with a few coppers a week. He called for those who refused to join the trade union movement to be ostracised, condemning them as anti-social and criminal.[30] Commenting on this, the *Jewish Chronicle* labour correspondent contended that what was needed was not force or discipline, but industrial education. He pointed to the failure of Jewish labour leaders to recognise the crucial differences between the Jewish and the English worker. "They forget that the Jewish proletariat is still in course of formation ... the Jewish workman has no local permanence anywhere ...even in the most tolerant countries he is a proletarian on sufferance". And he quoted the Jewish labour leader, Mr. Joseph Finn, who stated bitterly, "he is not even allowed to be sweated in peace". Jewish workers in general found it hard to organise stable trade unions, and things were so much harder for the Jewish bakers, where it was rare to find more than three or four employed in a bakery. Solidarity and strength depends on numbers. Only a minority of the native English bakery workers were organised this time, and this was primarily in enterprises so large as to be comparable to factories.

In his memoirs, written in 1937 but not published until 1956, Rudolf Rocker claimed that the strike had been won in a few weeks. "The label helped the Jewish bakers' union to get better conditions in their part of the trade; they were for a long time in advance of the conditions of the workers organized in the English Bakers' union" — a claim that the AUOB would certainly have disputed. He stated further that it added to the sense of their strength among the Jewish workers generally and "helped to prepare the way for the big general strike later against the sweating system".[31] This claim has been repeated by the historian William Fishman in his *East End Jewish Radicals 1875-1914*.

However, an examination of the columns of both the *Jewish Chronicle* and *the Journeymen Bakers Magazine* at the time of the strike shows not only that the strike failed, but that it also led to the temporary collapse of the union. The local Yiddish press *Die Naye Tsayt* and *Arbeter Fraynd* also bore witness to the failure of the strike and to the bitter disappointment for Jewish trade unionists, after initial confidence of an outstanding triumph, of this debacle. As Rocker's memoirs were compiled from memory over thirty years after the event, it seems likely that he had been so impressed by the initial successes of the strike that he forgot its ultimate defeat. Surprisingly, Rocker also failed to discuss the far longer and tougher strike of 1913 which won the Jewish bakers a reduction in hours, an increase in pay, and recognition of the union.

Overall, though, Rocker (1873-1958) was a remarkable figure. He was not Jewish, but could identify with the oppressed Jewish workers, learn their language, and become one of their respected leaders. An outstanding figure in the Jewish Anarchist movement, and in the Jewish labour movement, he not only edited the *Arbeter Fraynd*, but inspired and helped lead the great tailoring strike of 1912 to abolish the sweat-shop system. His claim "that all the Jewish trade unions in the East End, without exception, were started by the initiative of the Jewish Anarchists" has been supported by Fishman. Rocker was also one of the founders of the Jewish Workers' Circle (in whose premises the Jewish Bakers' Union was in later years to have its headquarters), a mutual benefit society which also played an important part in the social and educational life of the East End. It survived until 1985.

Chapter 8. The Court Case 1904

One of the factors in the failure of the 1904 strike was the loss of morale and the financial burden resulting from the East London Bakers' Union's unsuccessful case at the Court of Appeal. The union was appealing against Mr. Justice Grantham's refusal to grant an injunction to prevent the defendant, a Mr. Goldstein, selling bread with the union's label attached.

The Times covered this case at length in June 1904, and it tells us a great deal about the affairs of the union and conditions of its workers. The case came before the Court of Appeal on 8 June 1904 (Henn Collins, Master of the Rolls, Sterling and Matthew, Lord Justices): East London Bakers' Unions v. Goldstein.[1] The union was the proprietor of a copyright label which had been duly entered at Stationers' Hall on 25 September 1903. The copyright label consisted of a drawing of two bakers in a bakehouse, two loaves, and a peel and trough, and two cottage loaves with a motto, "Unity is strength. Union Bread for Union Men, East London Bakers' Union." The plaintiff union of 250 working bakers brought this action, alleging that the defendant had used the copyright label in connection with his business of baker without the sanction of the union, and after receiving an intimation from them that he was not authorised to use it. The union would appear to have grown markedly since the previous year, when it had only 100 members, two fifths of the number indicated in the report.[2] As the historian V. D. Lipman observed in his *Social History of the Jews in England, 1850-1950*, the "continually rising and falling, splitting and reuniting unions covered only a small portion of the Jewish workers. The membership of the unions fluctuated, and at a time of strike or lockouts might rise meteorically and then drop again a week or so after".[3]

According to *The Times*' report, an agreement between the plaintiff, the Jewish Bakers' Union, and the defendant, Mr. Goldstein, a master baker, had been signed on 17 May 1904. It was commonplace for a master baker's label to be affixed to each loaf of bread baked in many Jewish bakeries. In addition — or instead — a trade union label could be placed thereon. Mr. Goldstein had agreed that a trade union label be stuck on each loaf of bread. The working day was long – according to the agreement "12 hours shall be recognised as a term of work, every day, but on Thursday 2 hours extra".

The fact that Jewish bakeries were closed on Saturdays, and in the winter were open on Fridays for only half a day, meant that on

Thursday the Jewish bakers were busier than ever; and, if there was one night when an unemployed Jewish baker might be called upon to help out more than any other it would be a Thursday, or the evening prior to most Jewish holidays. Another condition of the agreement with Mr. Goldstein which the bakers insisted on was that "no overtime shall be worked on ordinary days except the day before a holiday" This was designed not merely to reduce excessive demands on the worker, but also meant that employment would be given to more workers — one of the admirable facets of the union was its unfailing concern for those in the trade who were unemployed. The condition regarding overtime was that "all overtime is to be paid at time and a half". In this respect things have changed little over the last century. In respect of wages, an important provision was that "no man is to be employed at a wage less than 26/- as a minimum." At this time more than half the adult workers were earning less than 30s. a week and a considerable percentage of these were living in conditions of poverty. However, compared with working-class wages in general, a baker earning this minimum would not fall into the category of the very poor, but would be in the "middle grades". Furthermore, Jewish bakery workers received a daily allowance of bread. In addition, the agreement with Mr. Goldstein stipulated "one man shall not do the work of another class, higher, or lower", and that "no master shall personally work as a baker".

However burdensome the working conditions, the agreement did guarantee: "one full day's rest in seven" — Saturday, the Jewish Sabbath. These bakeries were also closed on Jewish Holy days. There was no agreement in the early days of the union that there were any other holidays.

The agreement stipulated that "only members of the East London Jewish Bakers' Union shall be employed". The strength of the union was also demonstrated by the condition that "a delegate of the Union shall at any time be permitted to enter the bakehouse for Trade Union business". If a baker agreed to these terms he was entitled, subject to a payment of 5s. a year to the London Jewish Bakers' Union, to use the union label on bread baked in his bakery. The defendant accepted "that the trade union label is the property of the organisation mentioned above and can only be used by me with their consent. If the union's label is to be taken away from me, the reason for so doing must first be submitted to arbitration".

However, as *The Times* reported: "The plaintiffs alleged that the defendant also orally agreed not to enter into unfair competition with master bakers who were producing their bread under trade union conditions. They alleged that the defendant was selling bread at less than cost price, so as to ruin the trade of the master bakers who were paying trade union wages and that the result of permitting the defendant to use their label would be that the defendant would have a label, which he could impose on the public and ruin the trade of the masters who paid fair wages, and compel bakers to work at inadequate wages and under insanitary conditions. They further alleged that the affixing of the label to a loaf was a representation to the general public that the loaf was made by members of the East London Bakers' Union and with the sanction of the East London Bakers' Union, and that loaves baked by the defendant and exhibited and sold by him with the label attached were not baked by members of the East London Bakers' Union; and that there were not any members of the East London Bakers' Union in the defendant's employment. The plaintiffs, on commencing the action, applied for an injunction restraining the defendant from using the label until the trial of the action. The defendant denied the alleged oral agreement, and said that he was selling his bread at the same price as the majority of bakers in the East End of London, and that he was, and always had been, willing to pay the rate of wages and abide by the conditions set out in the above written agreement".

As to the plaintiff's claim that there was another agreement made orally (outside the written agreement) by which the defendant undertook not to compete unfairly with other masters, the Master of the Rolls said "no such undertaking was to be found in the written agreement and ...there was no foundation for the allegation of an oral agreement .... the injunction which the plaintiffs asked for would entirely destroy the defendant's trade ... the Court would not be justified in allowing an injunction to go having that effect and based on an allegation not made out. The defendant having undertaken ....to keep an account of all bread sold by him, to which the label was attached, the Appeal would be dismissed".

The plaintiffs had lost their case, but the significance of the judgment was that the Court of Appeal was prepared to look upon a local collective agreement as a contractual bargain. However, in the opinion of Professor Wedderburn, the judges did not really appreciate that they were dealing with a point of principle about collective agreements generally. The judgment was also cited in argument in a crucial case in 1969 between Fords, the engineers' union and the TGWU about the legal enforceability of collective agreements. Wedderburn, who was Counsel for the TGWU in that action, did not believe that the bakers' union case was particularly influential in deciding the legal status of modern collective agreements.4

London Jewish Bakers' Union Label (Original size 27 x 33mm)
Image supplied by Sid Kaufman

Chapter 9. A Battle on All Fronts

When the Executive Committee of the AUOB heard in January 1905[1] that the Jewish bakers in London had dissolved their union and returned £15 of the grant they had received from the AUOB during their recent strike, the "English" union may well have thought that that was the last to be heard of the matter. Indeed, as the *Jewish Chronicle* commented at the time, the announcement of the dissolution of a Jewish trade union was a rare occurrence. "Most of the Jewish trade societies die of sheer inanition".[2] The news of the end of the East London Bakers' Union was a surprise to many friends of Jewish labour. It also had a sad effect on the existing Jewish unions, especially since the agitation the previous year among the journeymen bakers had gained more general support than earlier struggles, and had initially achieved greater, albeit partial, gains. The *Jewish Chronicle* writer believed that the widespread public sympathy had led the union to imagine that all their demands would be conceded quickly, and therefore all overtures for compromise had been waved aside impatiently. When employers had started to use the trade union label regardless of the conditions attached to it, the union had embarked on legal action, "little aware of the intricacies of the law", and when the court had found unexpectedly in favour of the employers, "the faith in the registered label as the great hope of the Union's future was at once destroyed... Without a sufficiency of membership and the requisite sinews of war", dissolution remained the only possible course. However, the writer forecast that "after a few years the events of the past year will be quite forgotten". This prediction was fulfilled far more quickly than expected, for from the ruins of the East London Bakers' Union there arose the Jewish Bakers' and Confectioners' Union.[3] Although pleased to see this phoenix arising from the ashes, the *Chronicle's* labour correspondent was annoyed by the way this had happened, considering that "it would certainly have been more convenient and becoming" to have reorganised the old society rather than dissolve it and start a new one.

The resuscitated Jewish union's problems were complicated by an old issue which refused to go away, and which united both masters and men, especially in London - the question of Sunday baking. The 500 bakers in the London Master Bakers' Protection Society and the AUOB fought as one against both Jewish master bakers and the Jewish bakers' trade union in London. The ill feeling this issue engendered often expressed itself in more general anti-

Semitism. On 19 May 1905 a special House of Lords Committee heard evidence on the Sunday Closing (Shops) Bill. At that time, feeling on the question of Sunday opening ran deeply on both religious and economic grounds. Robert Seward, President of the London Master Bakers' Protection Society, gave the committee a history of the struggle against the Jewish baking industry on this matter. Seward made it clear that he spoke on behalf of all non-Jewish master bakers in the UK — all were vehemently opposed to the baking and delivery of bread on Sundays, and they contended that this was on the increase in London, especially among the Jews.

The master bakers' society first took cases of Sunday baking to court in 1876, and then again in 1883. In 1891 they tried to use the law in earnest, but magistrates imposed fines of merely 1s. and 5s. They protested to the Home Secretary over the pettiness of the fines, but to no avail. Of 57 summonses taken out in that year, there were 36 convictions, 4 dismissals and 17 cases were adjourned. The cost of these prosecutions was £170.

In 1902 the master bakers spent £485 on prosecutions and in the following year £192. They employed journeymen bakers to watch premises and follow horses and carts to gather evidence. But when the prosecutions stopped, the Jewish bakers made and sold more bread in and around London. Seward claimed that Jewish bakers made bread on Saturdays as well as on Sundays, and protested that this would force Christian bakers to do likewise. The small fines for breaking the law meant that Sunday baking was increasing, not only in London but also in places like Manchester, Liverpool, Bristol and Leeds. To avoid discovery when they knew their premises were being watched Jewish bakers, Seward complained, boarded them up or covered them with sacks. Only a change in the law could cope with the problem of Sunday baking.[4]

In response, the Jewish Master Bakers' Association organised a petition against the threat of a Bill to prohibit Sunday trading, with the support of the Whitechapel and Spitalfields Male and Female Costermongers, the Street Sellers' Union and by the Jewish inhabitants of Stepney at large.[5] Meanwhile, the Select Committee of the Lords sympathised with those who obeyed the law and lost business as a result.

In the AUOB's *Journeymen Bakers Magazine* for April 1906, John Jenkins attacked attempts by the London Committee of the Board of Deputies of British Jews to amend the law, so that the Jewish Community should he permitted to trade on Sunday.

Jenkins' language was so extreme as to suggest that he was motivated as much by anti-Semitism as anything else: "A small army of solicitors and barristers were engaged in the attempt to stem the tide of the ever grasping Israelite", he wrote, appealing for action "to arrest this modern tendency to further enslave a very considerable portion of society to the baneful effects of what may prove to be, if uncontested, a moral disaster to the community". Jenkins concluded: "formerly it was in the East End only where Sunday trading was rife, but not content with supplying their religious compatriots of the ghetto, they have invaded the West End with their Sunday morning fresh-made bread to the detriment of the British bakers who are handicapped by these unscrupulous traders".6 Speaking at the Hammersmith branch of the AUOB Jenkins went even further: "the foreign Jew baker should be compelled to leave the Country if he could not conform to the law of the Country of his adoption".

While the perennial struggle over the Sunday baking dispute persisted, dividing Jewish and non-Jewish master bakers as well as their journeymen employees, the revived Jewish Bakers' Union in London had other obstacles to overcome. A general problem for all Jewish trade unionism was the tendency of recent Jewish immigrants to leave Britain after a short stay and continue on to the USA or Canada. As a report in the *Jewish Chronicle* in July 1905 put it: "Most of the past labour leaders, indeed all who were capable of impressing the multitudes, are now residents of USA". Among the long list of those who have forsaken England were names like Benjamin Feigenbaum, "a platform orator of great power and a prolific labour journalist ... one of the first to start Jewish trade union and labour organisations", Morris Winchevsky, who was associated with him, S. Yanovsky "an agitator of advanced views", recently S. Ellstein, the Jewish Bakers' leader, and earlier still his brother L. Ellstein, past organiser of the Leeds Jewish tailoresses. "No wonder", the reporter concluded, "that the Jewish labour movement should now be utterly devoid of enthusiasm and constantly relapsing into disorganisation and indifference."7

England's loss was USA's gain. A powerful strike among Jewish bakers in New York resulted in "tens of thousands of poor Hebrews .... without bread".8 Commenting on the low numbers of Jewish delegates at the TUC, the *Jewish Chronicle* labour correspondent suggested that "Anti-alien, in reality, anti-Jewish outbreaks among trade unionists" may well be attributable to "the disinclination of Jewish workers to mix with their English confreres on every possible occasion", and expressed the hope that Jewish workers would see "the advantages in future of being represented at the Congress".[9] Two months later, however, the paper was not impressed by the militant demands of a meeting at the "Wonderland" in Whitechapel, which included a general strike to begin on 1 May 1906.[10] Its reporter scorned the "cheap rhetoric" which was "the delight of the youthful immigrants from Russia". Such a tactic was not only impracticable among the "imperfectly constituted and unorganized proletariat of East London", but also practically unknown among English trade unionists and fraught with the gravest consequences. The Jewish workers of the East End were being "exploited by propagandists of every imaginable fad" – the *Arbeter Fraynd* and the anarchists met particular disapproval from the *Jewish Chronicle*.

The year 1906 began with successes for the Jewish labour movement – a victory for the boot and shoe workers[11] and a successful tailors' strike. The strike movement was spreading both throughout London and in the provinces and, as the *Jewish Chronicle* put it, "hardly a week passes without a fresh strike breaking out in one or other of the trades in which Jewish workers are engaged ... the number of strikes within the last four months is quite phenomenal compared with any previous period in the history of the Jewish labour movement". The clothing trade and furnishing trade were in ferment and "the Jewish journeymen bakers are again to the fore calling for 'justice and rights".[12] While only a few months earlier the paper had scorned the efforts of the anarchists, it admitted that "the increasing strike movement ...may be directly traced to the advance propaganda" – i.e. of the anarchists.[13] The East End Jewish workmen appeared "to have undergone a process of transformation". Indifference and submission had been replaced by courage, independence and a determination to secure freedom and humane treatment, and "with an increase in their membership the Jewish trade unions feel enabled to enforce their demands upon the employers". This change was connected with the arrival of new immigrants "fresh from the scenes of an heroic struggle for liberty entailing enormous self sacrifice", (i.e. the 1905 revolution in Russia), and to the continued influx of persecuted Jews who brought with them a new spirit of militancy. By mid-March, according to the *Jewish Chronicle*, "strikes are now the order of the day with victories for the mantle makers, the cap makers and the embroidery workers".[14]

The re-established Jewish Bakers' Union had become imbued with a new spirit of enthusiasm and a determination to demonstrate that it was not behind other unions. I. Caplan, who had led the union in the strike of 1900, was back as its secretary. Once again it was the question of the trade union label which inspired action. The union claimed, "with some measure of fairness", that a number of the master bakers had been placing the label on the loaves without justification and were not in fact employing trade union labour or paying the trade union rate.[15] The winter of 1905-6 saw a massive influx of Jewish workers into the various trade unions, which was vital because so many Jews were exploited in the sweated industries. Sweating, however, was a practice that was widespread irrespective of religion or nationality. Reporting the "Daily News Sweated Industries Exhibition" then taking place in London, the *Jewish Chronicle* stressed that neither the tailoring trade nor the Jews were responsible for the worst instances of sweating. "The vilest sweating is committed in the sacred name of the Christian religion. The worst paid work shown in the Exhibition is that of making confirmation wreaths".[16]

June and July 1906 saw feverish activity among the Jewish trade unions, the outstanding struggle being a strike among the tailors. Grievances which would have previously been regarded as minor, could now spark off strike action and, for example, when a master baker was accused of insulting a Jewish journeyman baker, his comrades stopped work. When the masters' society supported its member the union accused it of provocative measures, and decided to take up any and every challenge. Matters looked likely to escalate. From Spring 1906 the Jewish Bakers' Union, under its energetic and experienced new secretary, had fought a series of battles with the masters — at times violent — which were reported in the non-Jewish as well as the Jewish press. The union was at a disadvantage in that it could not afford paid officers, and was too poor to have built up a general strike fund. Furthermore, although the other Jewish unions were sympathetic, they could not help financially, as they themselves were widely embroiled in bitter and costly conflict with their own masters.

The union decided to abandon the "old and worn out method" of attacking all the bakehouses at once, because that tactic had been losing it public sympathy. It was also a major task "to keep the wolf of starvation" from the door of the strikers' families when the union was in a general and prolonged strike. So, as the *Jewish Chronicle* put it, the men chose "the method of guerrilla warfare attacking the bakehouses singly, and isolating the enemy as it were".[17] In this way, the support of the general public was retained and the majority of bakers (who remained in employment) were able and willing to maintain the strikers on the principle of mutual aid. The employers took counter-measures to foil the union. They threatened to close bakehouses, to lock out their men, to engage non-union and non-Jewish labour and to resort to legal action in cases involving physical violence. Each side accused the other of intimidation and malpractice. Two outstanding cases ended up in the courts, involving master bakers in Hanbury Street and in Brick Lane.[18]

This particular Hanbury Street employer was regarded as the scourge of the strikers. He was credited with having smashed the union in the past, and he made no secret of his determination to do so again. He was described as "more than a match for the union officials", who were "at their wits ends as to how to get the upper hand in their negotiations with him". To try to bring this employer to his knees, the union distributed handbills and posted them on windows calling on all workers to oppose him and boycott his products. It accused him of refusing to employ Jewish labour and claimed that he employed someone who had caused eight people to be deported to Siberia. A man who had been haranguing a crowd in the vicinity of this bakery, smashed its shop window. He was arrested and released on bail. He then issued a counter summons for assault against the master baker, who, in turn, took out 10 summonses against members of the union.

The second incident involved a middle-aged master Jewish baker, who complained that he had been threatened that he "would be stretched out flat", that his daughter had been subject to menaces, and that his wife had been harried to her death by similar treatment. The union's quarrel with him was not for employing non-Jewish labour, but for using non-union labour. The master was upset by the agitation against him and by calls for a boycott, but it is likely that his wife's recent death had led him to exaggerate the actions of the union.

Both masters and union tried to enlist the sympathies of the Jewish press. For example, H. M. Cohen, a master baker of Umberston Street, Commercial Road, published a long letter, detailing the generous scale of wages he said he paid and claimed his men worked an average of 11 hours a day. He complained of bad debts of customers, incompetence and insolence of workers and threats by workers to customers.[19] The union disputed these claims.

The *East London Advertiser* enjoyed publishing detailed reports of court cases arising from strife between Jewish employers and their employees.[20] On one occasion, the paper alleged, 500 people surrounded a baker's shop and molested his customers, while on another as many as 1500-2000 supporters of the journeymen bakers congregated outside Slaters' bakershop in Crellin Street, broke its windows and attacked his customers. According to the police, on that occasion a Yiddish leaflet was being circulated which accused Slater of aiming at starving Jewish workers. "The scoundrel ...wants to wear out the last bit of flesh off our legs. We are not the starters but the ones who have been started on. Slaters in James Street are no longer employing Union men". Sentences on the men ranged from fines to imprisonment with up to three months hard labour for charges including intimidation, watching and besetting, breaking windows, and assaulting policemen.

So bitter was the strife — a man aged 70 died after a blow on the head, although this was almost certainly an accident — that there were attempts to have the dispute referred to arbitration. However, although a majority on each side were amenable, the attempts came to nothing.[21] The Jewish Bakers' Union rejected charges that they were unprepared to work with their non-Jewish confreres. At a meeting of Jewish cabinet makers held at Christchurch Hall, Hanbury Street, speakers on a mixed Jewish and non-Jewish platform referred to the desperate plight of the Jewish bakers in the East End and noted that "the more intelligent classes of the population" did not believe the charges of racial antagonism on the part of Jewish bakers towards non-Jewish bakers.[22]

While the union was prepared to accept arbitration on the charge that they were unwilling to work alongside non-Jewish employees, the masters were not ready to agree that the locked-out men should be re-instated, even on the old conditions. They insisted that no re-instatement could be considered until after the arbitrators' final award. Matters came to a head when a leading employer advertised a reduction in the price of bread and asserted that the strike had been settled. This premature, untrue, statement led to negotiations being suspended. The union declared that they would agree to arbitration only in respect of those employers who publicly withdrew the calumny that the union was opposed to the employment of non-Jews. It also rejected arbitration with any employer who had misled the public by claiming the strike was settled, and with those masters whose actions had led to workers receiving three-month prison sentences.[23] After dragging on for some time the struggle of the men petered out. Both sides had suffered morally and financially, but it was the workers who, through sheer exhaustion, eventually caved in, and work resumed on the old conditions.

One of the problems the bakehouse workers faced was highlighted in an article by Joseph Finn, published in the *Jewish Chronicle* on 5 October 1906, examining the sweating system. It pointed out that trade unionism — the strongest defence against such exploitation — was ineffectual in the underdeveloped industries in which Jewish workmen were employed, where the master of today had himself been a workman yesterday. It cited the example of the mantle makers' trade, where 90% of the then masters had once been members of the Mantle Makers' Union. Exactly the same considerations applied to the Jewish baking trade at that time. Only with the development of the factory system, which would bring together large numbers of workers under one roof would the workers be ripe for trade unionism.

Towards the end of 1906 fresh trouble arose involving a very well-known employer, Morris Rosenberg of 54 Commercial Road, who had "extensive experience in economic warfare" and had "figured in every Jewish strike in the past except the last".[24] Early in the spring his workers had won a pay rise of 20%, which brought their wages up to 30s. a week. Consequently, Rosenberg's employees had not been involved in the strike. However, his workers charged that he had decided to reduce their wages to their former level of 25s. Rosenberg in turn denied this, and complained that the union was interfering in the management of his affairs, trying to force on him "jobbers" or unskilled labour. Furthermore, Rosenberg was suing Mr. Caplan, the secretary of the Jewish Bakers' Union, for libel over a handbill issued by the union and signed by him. Caplan, who pleaded justification, was a colourful and charismatic figure in the world of Jewish labour. He had an extensive and varied experience of Jewish trade unionism — in addition to leading the Jewish bakers he was also secretary of the Cap Makers' Union, which at that time was trying to set up a co-operative producing cloth hats and caps. (This enterprise, like previous attempts to set up bakers', tailors' or cigarette makers' co-operatives, ended in failure.)

Caplan was a well-known and accomplished platform speaker, who, it was said, had previously been a Jewish itinerant preacher. He was certainly well versed in Talmudic lore, and frequently used illustrations from that source in his speeches.[25] However, he had long since abandoned his religious beliefs and become "an ardent advocate of drastic changes in society from which even advanced radicals would shrink". Cap makers, tailors, journeymen bakers –

Caplan had led them all in desperate struggles to improve their conditions.

The libel case against Caplan ended early in 1907, when he withdrew his statements and apologised to Rosenberg. Commenting on this case, the *Jewish Chronicle* castigated Jewish labour leaders for their recklessness in rushing into print and warned them to guard against making loose and offensive statements when drawing up handbills for publication.[26] However, Caplan's popularity in Jewish labour circles was unaffected. In August 1907 he became secretary of the Cigarette Makers', Tobacco Cutters' and Strippers' Union in August 1907, and it is unlikely that he was influenced by the *Chronicle*'s hopes that he would forsake "doubtful methods" for "moderation as a surer method of settling labour disputes".[27] The paper was never slow to offer advice to Jewish workers on their efforts to improve their conditions. Moderation, conciliation, arbitration were its watchwords. It also urged Jewish workers to seek naturalisation, although it recognised that the high cost was four or five times the weekly wage of an employed worker. It tried to win the support of the Labour Party ("becoming an increasing quantity in the State") for reducing the cost of naturalisation.[28] At that stage, few realised how important this new party would become.

Despite the sufferings of the Jewish poor, England was a safe haven for them. Pogroms against their fellow Jews were still prevalent in the Russian Empire, and the Social Democratic Federation at its annual conference in Carlisle resolved to organise a mass meeting in the East End of London against this persecution. Herbert Burrows proposed, and H. M. Hyndman seconded, the conference motion expressing horror and indignation at "the atrocities which are continually being perpetrated by the autocratic despotism of Russia on a large section of the Russian people and especially on the Jewish race".[29] Although the lives of the Jews in England were not threatened, their livelihoods continued to be precarious. But the heady struggles of 1906 had become a thing of the past and trade unionism was at a low ebb. There were few reports in the Jewish press on activity to improve their conditions. By early 1908, even a perennial optimist like Rudolf Rocker was bewailing the resistance of the Jewish labour movement, both in the East End of London and in the country at large against any attempt to organise its forces.[30] The response to May Day 1908, which "evoked only a faint echo as compared to previous years", reflected the disorganised state of the Jewish labour unions.[31] By 1909 even the column heading "Labour

News" had disappeared from the *Jewish Chronicle*, although this may have been because of a change in editorial policy.

However, the movement was not dead. On 30 May 1909 between 2—3000 journeymen bakers and supporters demonstrated in Trafalgar Square in support of the Bakers' [8 hours] Bill then before Parliament. In the meantime they demanded a 54-hour working week with a minimum weekly wage of 30s. for all adults working in bakehouses. Members of the Jewish Bakers' Union took part in this demonstration. Even if the union was not exactly flourishing, it was still alive, as an item included in the September issue of the *Journeymen Bakers Magazine* attested: "Many of the Jewish bakers in the East End of London are exhibiting in their shop windows certificates of membership of the London Jewish Bakers' Union. The employers bind themselves to employ only union members; to work not more than 12 hours a day, and six days a week, and to abolish Saturday work".32

Neither the Jewish Bakers' Union nor the London District of the Amalgamated Union were recruiting well at this time, and to make matters worse, differences between these unions frequently assumed major proportions. There was a running acrimonious dispute between the two unions, reported in the *Journeymen Bakers Magazine* between November 1909 and September 1911. It was mainly about the ever-present question of "poaching". The Jewish union was aggrieved when the AUOB London District accepted members it had expelled. This was made worse still when such members were used, according to the Jewish union, as strike breakers. Conflict reached such a height that a representative of the Jewish union warned that it would fight against its brother union and it would be "knife or life",33 while Jacob Jung, leader of the No. 26 (German) branch of the AUOB and a leading critic of the Jewish Bakers' Union, said, "In peace we must not work in their shops; in war we must not fill their places".34 The London District of the AUOB referred angrily to "the ever-recurring Jewish question" and of having "more than our share of trouble with the Jews".35

Mr. Sharp and Mr. Jenkins, the heads of the respective unions, were unable to resolve their differences, and the dispute was eventually referred to the General Federation of Trade Unions and the Parliamentary Committee of the TUC. The former body was established in 1898. It embraced any trade union which desired to affiliate to it, and still exists today as a body for smaller, specialist trade unions. It sought to settle industrial differences peaceably, and one of its main functions was to mediate in disputes between its affiliate bodies. The Jewish union even asked the London Trades Council to help resolve the dispute. In fact, both unions had been guilty of intransigence and of using intemperate language, and when the protracted quarrel ended, blame was apportioned by all the arbitrating bodies more or less evenly between them.36 Grave problems faced all journeymen bakers, and internecine strife did not help.

In 1910, a new column "From The East End" began to appear in the *Jewish Chronicle*. On 10 June 1910, its columnist wrote, "Trouble again in the ranks of the Jewish journeymen bakers! I thought that the placing of the magic trade union label on every English loaf and chola disposed once and for all of the dissensions of the past. But no! 150 workers declared their intention last week to strike".37 Two weeks later a master baker, J. Cohen of 57 Umberston Street, Commercial Road, wrote complaining that the Jewish master bakers disliked the label, which they saw as an infringement of their liberties,38 and in the following issue, the columnist complained that the strike meant a loss of trade for Jewish bakers, because non-Jewish bakers "were stepping in and making hay while the sun shines". One master baker explained that using the label was not only "unhygienic" but also involved extra cost and labour for the employer. The labels had to be bought from the union and they were numbered to control the quantity of loaves baked. He claimed that the men also demanded to see the master's books and check the number of loaves and labels. The employers resorted to employing non-Jewish labour to circumvent this. The *Chronicle* also mocked the "ridiculous importance attached to the label". In the East End "every two penny-ha'penny baker affixes his portrait to every loaf he sends out, and on each side of this man's portrait is the man's name and address and the town from which he originally came". It was carrying "the free portrait business too far when the loaf carried a brace of labels — that is the union's and the individual master baker's label".39

There was no report of the outcome of the strike. The columnist "From The East End" was more concerned to entertain than inform. However, in mid-1912 this column was replaced by a new one: "With the Children of the Ghetto", which marked a change from flippancy and pomposity to sympathetic interest towards the plight of the Jewish workers and the struggle of Jewish trade unions in London's East End.

Chapter 10. 1913: "The Ghetto Anticipated Them All"

The second decade of the 20th century opened with gigantic industrial struggles of seamen and dockers, followed by transport workers and miners. Troops were used in the big strikes. A "great unrest" or general spirit of revolt was sweeping through the working class. It affected nearly every branch of industry and led to decisive advances in trade unionism. Jewish workers too were touched by this ferment. In July 1912 the *Jewish Chronicle* reported protest meetings by shop assistants, barbers and others, and commented: "unionism is going strong down here now. Every worker is discerning the utility of combination from the costermonger to the tailor's presser. And why not?"1

There was particular unrest among the tailors. The columnist writing "With the Children of the Ghetto" commented caustically on "sleek master tailors, their bejewelled spouses, and their beautiful homes, all wrung out of men and women who demand nothing greater than a fair wage and decent conditions of labour ... The present unrest in the labouring world is a wholehearted attempt to right wrongs of long standing. The striking tailors are making heavy sacrifices. One hopes they will reap the benefit".2 Women, too, were involved in struggle, with remarkable solidarity shown by Jewish female garment workers in the West End.3

It was not long before the bakers rejoined the struggle for shorter hours and better wages. As a *Jewish Chronicle* correspondent observed in August 1912, "there is much to ponder in the statement [that] by reducing the hours of the baker to eight a day the price of bread would only increase by one-sixth of a penny for a four pound loaf".4 Nonetheless, at the start of 1913, the *Journeymen Bakers Magazine* published a pessimistic review of recent years which concluded that the prospect of the journeyman baker getting a fair reward "if not hopeless, is very uphill work indeed". The review blamed the workers' mental apathy. The starvation wages and deplorable conditions were a disgrace to London and to civilisation. A journeyman baker could work anything up to 90 hours a week for a wage a street-sweeper could earn working nine- or even eight-hour days. Without an Act of Parliament, only downing tools would force the employer to make concessions. "The question is: has the London operative baker the pluck to do this? If he acts upon it he wins; if not his present slavery will continue indefinitely".5 A report in the same issue, however, showed that some Jewish workers did have the necessary pluck. The London District Board of the AUOB in

December 1912 resolved that two of their own non-Jewish members should cease work at a certain shop where the Jewish union had called a strike.

Unfortunately, such examples of solidarity did not mean an end to all disagreements between the AUOB and the LJBU on Sunday working, poaching, blacklegging or even the "platform", i.e. the charter of rights each union championed. It took months of negotiation and the aid of both the GFTU and TUC before a dispute about AUOB members strikebreaking in "Jewish shops" was resolved in favour of the Jewish union.

While this was going on, the AUOB had also been engaged in a strike with the master bakers. It ended with an agreement which the LJBU also signed, that in factories (where there were more than 6 employees and machinery was driven by power) there was to be a 54-hour week and the wages of the lowest operative was to be 32s. a week, while in bakehouses there was to be a 60-hour week and the lowest wage was fixed at 30s. a week.[6]

Meanwhile, the Jewish bakers' own struggle was coming to a head, as they presented the masters with an ultimatum that their demands be met by 28 April, the seventh day of Passover. The *Jewish Chronicle*, which had reported the struggle sympathetically, began to take a more hostile line. Noting that the journeymen had asked for and got the 12-hour day, paid Jewish holidays, and the affixing of the trade union label to union-made bread, its writer proceeded to poke fun at the journeymen's platform — "a weird and wonderful document". It demanded a nine-hour day (including an hour for meals) and a changing room. "What next!" spluttered one little baker. "If they wait long enough they shall have my front parlour to change in and the use of my piano. Where is it all going to end?" The paper was clearly beginning to sympathise with the master baker, not least over the question of the label — "a most interesting production in Yiddish and English. In the centre there is a portrait of the baker himself, either in skull cap, 'bowler', or with no hat at all. The no-hatted baker is shunned by the ultra-orthodox ... around the portrait by way of a frame is the baker's name, the years he has been established, the province from which he hails, and the legend that the bread is of 'bonified' trade union manufacture".[7]

Informed that the LJBU was contemplating strike action from 29 April if the Jewish masters did not concede their demands, the London District Board of the AUOB agreed to withdraw their men from shops in dispute and on 3 May a 3000-strong procession took place in support of the Jewish journeymen bakers.[8] Other Jewish trade unions had voluntarily levied themselves, resulting in a gift of over £160. Similar levies were promised weekly until victory was won. The meeting following the procession pledged moral and financial support and only to purchase bread which was baked in a trade union shop. The AUOB London District Board showed its solidarity when, of six of its union members working in Jewish shops during the dispute, four stopped when ordered and two were expelled.[9]

The strike received a lot of coverage in the Jewish press. It was claimed that 250 to 300 men were striking, with 4-5000 men in support, although the first figure was probably exaggerated.[10] In response to the union's platform for a 9-hour day, including an hour off for dinner, the masters expressed willingness to concede an 11-hour day. Later leaflets issued by the union substituted a demand for a 10-hour day. To support their case for the longer working day, the masters pointed to the ways in which Jewish baking differed from non-Jewish. In the Jewish bakehouse a lot of time was wasted while the men waited for the brown bread which took longer to rise. In addition there was more fancy bread made in Jewish bakeries and this took up more time. In all types of bakehouses time was lost for ovens to get hotter or cooler. The masters argued that if they accepted the demand for a nine-hour day including a dinner hour, with at least another hour a day lost for other reasons, this would mean only seven hours a day would be worked, and the masters could not make an adequate profit on that basis. If the Jewish master bakers were forced in that case to increase their prices, they claimed, then the public would turn to the non-Jewish bakers and Jewish journeymen bakers would be in an even worse plight. The masters also pointed out that, in addition to their pay, each man got a quartern or a quartern and a half of bread per day as well as a quartern of flour a day. While they were prepared to concede the minimum 32s. for 3rd and 4th hands, they were not prepared to relieve the men of the duty of carrying the bread upstairs from underground bakeries as it would mean the employment of an extra man for that purpose alone. As for the demand for 9d per hour for jobbers and 1s. for fancy bakers, the masters were willing to pay no more than the rate of the non-Jewish unions. The "ultimatum" of the men that only *bona fide* trade unionists be employed and that the trade union label be used on all bread was also a sticking point. The masters claimed they would lose those customers who objected to the label.

For his part, the *Jewish Chronicle* reporter contended that the situation of the Jewish journeyman baker compared favourably with that of his non-Jewish comrade, and that the men's solidarity put the union in a strong position, given the disloyalty among the masters, some of whom had given in to the men to capture their rivals' trade. The claim for a special room for men to change their clothes was already covered by LCC bye-laws, and the reporter seemed to think that conditions were not as bad as the men suggested and "do not seem to warrant the high-handed attitude they have been advised to adopt".[11] The paper observed that the May Day 1913 demonstration was "a great day for the bakers", and that there was "a great cortege" of Jewish socialists, women as well as men, who had their own platform with Yiddish speakers at Hyde Park. The reporter sniffed that "many were in their Sabbath array and not a few wore gloves, just as do the wives of the 'bloated capitalists' of whom the socialists speak so scornfully". Sartorial elegance, it appeared, was not something for the lower orders.

The strike dragged on for months, with neither side willing to come to terms. Inevitably the hardships aroused feelings of frustration and bitterness. Some workers resorted to tactics which landed them in court. In one case (dismissed for lack of evidence) two men were accused of sprinkling paraffin over a Berner Street baker's newly baked bread — the master baker had employed non-union labour.[12] There was another case against a man for preventing customers from entering a baker's shop and in a third the accused was fined for knocking bread bought from a baker's shop on strike out of women's hands. The local East London press, which was rarely reluctant to print stories that might fuel anti-Semitism, gave much space to such incidents in their weekly "Courts' reports". For its part, the *Jewish Chronicle* charged that nine out of ten of those involved in these conflicts were "self-avowed anarchists" who are "being taught a useful lesson but are taking the lesson to heart all too slowly".

Unfortunately, the initial sympathy of the non-Jewish bakers was also being rapidly eroded. The AUOB rejected claims that non-Jewish trade unionists were strikebreaking in Jewish shops, even though these claims had been shown to have some substance when the matter had been raised with the TUC. Both unions accused each other of "poaching" members. Once again, the Jewish union tried to establish a co-operative bakery, and the AUOB accused the co-operative both of employing Jews to the exclusion of the members of the national union, and of making them work unlimited hours below the union rate.[13] To boost its members' meagre strike pay, the Jewish bakers rented two small bakeries in Brick Lane in the East End of London, where members worked making loaves on a rota basis. Additionally, one of the members hawked the bread so produced through the streets among the local Jewish population, calling on housewives to buy only bread baked by union labour. His call: "Koyf union broyt, vaybele" [Buy Union bread, wives] earned him the nickname of Moishe Union Broyt [Morris Unionbread]. In later years he appeared frequently in the union minutes, generally as Moishe Unionbread rather than under his own real name!

By early September there was still no sign of either side caving in. The *Jewish Chronicle* worried that the Jewish baking trade would be crippled, and that bread supply would be taken over by non-Jewish bakers. This raised the dread prospect of life without bagels, chollahs, platzels and rye bread, or of inferior products baked by non-Jewish firms.[14] One such firm did indeed advertise in Yiddish and English that its chollahs were delivered weekly.

The bakers' strike was not unique in East London, except in its length and bitterness. There were industrial upheavals across Britain in 1913. The Jewish garment workers, for example, that year won a working day of 8 am to 8 pm with one-and-a-half hours for meals, and the right of an authorised union official to enter a workshop at any reasonable time.

By 3 October 1913 the *Jewish Chronicle* reported the end of the strike – "the almost starved Jewish strikers started going to work immediately".[15] B. Verby of the *Jewish Express* had played a key part in securing a settlement after several weeks of trying to persuade masters and men to agree. The union had started the year with 200 members, and finished it with 192. However, as a result of the six months' strike it had won "one hour less a day, an increase of wages of 3s a week, payment for holidays and recognition of the Union".[16] It had raised £213 from street collections and concerts, and had received a grant of £200 from the General Federation of Trade Unions, and £645 from other unions. It had paid out over £1000 to the 180 union members involved in the dispute, and had spent about £26 on bread to be distributed to striking members. Although its own funds had been depleted by the strike, the union showed solidarity with striking bakers in Manchester and Leeds, donating £10 to the former and £5 to the latter.[17]

In London, the synagogue authorities had kept aloof from the strike. The columnist on "With the Children of the Ghetto" expressed surprise at this, and called upon the synagogue to "step down from its pedestal and identify itself more with the Jewish labouring masses". It was not enough to offer tickets gratis for the New Year services and to hold special Saturday afternoon services. Acidly he remarked: "The preacher may become gracefully rhetorical over the bread of affliction, but with the real bread of affliction in this year of grace he has no concern. Worldly disputes such as these are quite outside his own circle".[18] A quite different approach was seen in Manchester, for example, where there was "a spirit of trade unionism ... among the members of the Manchester Jewish congregation". One synagogue there was always at the disposal of a Jewish labour leader "for a discussion on Jewish trade unionism and Jewish labour in general", whereas in London the pulpits "had been used to denounce the combination of Jewish workmen". The columnist cited cases where Jewish institutions had gone out of their way to undermine the struggle of Jewish workers on strike, and concluded that Jewish ecclesiastical leaders could only hope to reach the hearts of the people if they were to "befriend the oppressed, plead the cause of the downtrodden worker".[19]

It was not only the Jewish press which followed this dispute. The six-month strike and its outcome received coverage both in the trade papers and in the national press. On 10 October 1913 the trade paper, the *Baker and Confectioner* referred to a recent report of the strike in the *Daily Herald*, which had welcomed the victory of the Jewish bakers and had written, "If trade unionists did their duty, labelling of trade union goods and boycotting of blackleg goods would be of great power. If no-one drank beer in any public-house where the bar workers were not in a Union, do you not think the disgraceful hours worked in public houses would be shortened?" The *Baker and Confectioner* was unconvinced, though, and observed, "Why, there is hardly a trade union leader who enquires whether his clothes are made by a staunch trade unionist or only by poor sweated Jews. He is just as indifferent about everything he eats and drinks".[20]

Chapter 11. 1914-1939

In the first half of 1914, despite the agreement that the National Union had concluded with the employers, workers in the bakery trade were still working excessive hours for low pay.[1] For all its superior resources and comparatively large membership, the AUOB faced the same problems as the tiny Jewish union when it came to dealing with small master bakers with very few employees. In these enterprises it was hard to make headway, and nearly all Jewish bakeries were run by small masters. Not long after the outbreak of war the national union's leader lamented that "most, if not all trades, have obtained considerable advance in wage rates and reduction in working hours, (but) the average working baker ... has gained very little as a result of the money spent and the work done by the Amalgamated Union, to improve the position".[2]

However, despite their common problems the AUOB and the insignificant Jewish union were unable to sink their differences. As the AUOB London District secretary complained in August 1914. "Our relations with the Jewish Bakers' Union are very uncertain.[3] The AUOB Annual Conference at Leicester on 3—4 August 1914, unanimously carried a resolution "viewing with alarm the prospect of a European war". But the London delegates were more preoccupied with Jewish bakers who were allegedly unwilling to allow non-Jews to work in a Jewish area. The *Journeymen Bakers Magazine* reported this under the heading "The trouble with the Jews".[4] For its part, the AUOB executive tried to smooth away difficulties, and a Manchester delegate made the well-intentioned, if somewhat patronising appeal that "it is our place to make them [the Jews] good and sound trade unionists".

Most members of the Jewish union were of foreign origin and would not, therefore, have been conscripted during the war. Although the Jewish union continued to submit its annual financial return, and the AUOB continued to publish the *Journeymen Bakers Magazine*, both unions seemed to be just ticking over. The total membership of the Jewish union did not change markedly between the beginning of 1914 and the end of 1916 when it was 185, although by the end of the war it had fallen to 136. During the war, the union continued to be affiliated to the TUC, to the General Federation of Trade Unions and to the Stepney Trades Council. In 1916 the return referred to the existence of a section of the union in Manchester, which paid contributions to London. Possibly some members had left London for Manchester during the war.

The lack of press reports of Jewish trade unionism is not surprising. Separate Jewish trade unionism was feasible and even necessary as long as the Jew was a person apart, economically, culturally, and linguistically, not wanted as a fellow unionist by the English worker. This position had been changing, so that even before the end of Great War, separate Jewish trade unions had ceased to exist even in the field where they had been strongest, namely tailoring.[5] Following the Trade Board Acts of 1909 a new union of tailors, the Tailors' and Garment Workers' Trade Union, had been created, and after the Jewish union in London had struck in sympathy with the non-Jewish tailors, it amalgamated with this new union. As more and more Jewish workers became Anglicised, soon the only separate unions were the Jewish printing union, which printed Yiddish newspapers and periodicals (and with the decline of Yiddish and the decreasing demand for any Yiddish newspapers their day was almost over), and the Jewish bakers' union for workers in bakehouses producing specialised types of Jewish bread.

For most of the 1920s the membership of the union did not exceed 129.[6] At that time, according to Mr. Grodzinski, there were around 35 Jewish bakeries (by the mid-1970s this number had declined to 15).[7] To help form a picture of the conditions in the inter-war period, in addition to press reports, we also have the personal reminiscences of former members of the Jewish bakers' union, Morris Cohen and J. Middleburgh, who joined the union in the early 1920s and the 1930s respectively, and much of the following is based on their recollections. The membership prior to the Second World War was still concentrated in the Aldgate, Whitechapel and Mile End areas of East London. The older members of the union were immigrants, mainly from Russia, Poland and Lithuania, and they normally still spoke Yiddish. Even the younger English-speaking members knew Yiddish.

From 1924 till 1940 the union's premises were at 51 Walden Street, London E1. At that time members were supposed to work no more than an 11-hour-day (or night) for six days a week but longer hours were frequently worked, especially on Thursday night. Michael Prooth, the union's secretary at the time of the General Strike, had been a "walking delegate" of the union, walking from bakery to bakery to ensure that members were not exceeding 11 hours a day. Morris Cohen recalled that in the years before the war the minimum wage was 1s 6d per hour, but J. Middleburgh remembered wages being lower. He recalled a strike in the 1930s for a closed shop. When women came to buy bread and were told it had been baked by scab labour, they reacted by throwing it back into the shop. Apparently with in a week the strike was successful.

At peak periods, when there was too much for the normal labour force to cope with, or if a worker was absent, there was an agency named Levy, used by both Jewish and non-Jewish employers and bakery workers, that supplied "jobbers". In addition to their wages, regular Jewish bakers received a bread allowance: two loaves a day plus four chollahs — special loaves baked for the Sabbath — on Friday. This was of considerable importance before the Second World War, when bread was still the staple food in many workers' homes. Sometimes the employers would give the baker cakes, and about once a fortnight union members would receive four pounds of flour from their employers.

For the most part, bakery workers were not involved in the general strike of May 1926. At the Annual Conference of the AUOB later that year its General Secretary, Mr. Banfield reported that "During the General Strike we were very careful to instruct our members to stay at work and the only dispute that arose was that of J. Lyons and Company".[8] Here three shop stewards had been dismissed and the TGWU called its members out. The bakers did not want to be seen as blacklegging in this situation, and bakery workers were called out even though, as expected, they lost.

As for the Jewish journeymen bakers, if the conduct of their secretary Prooth reflected the mood of the membership, they would have been only too eager to play their part in the general strike. Morris Cohen recalled him riding a white horse during the general strike[9] and his activities were reported in an issue of the *Jewish Chronicle* and at considerable length in both the *East London Advertiser* and the *East London Observer*[10] as well as in the national dailies and the trade papers. Prooth appeared at Thames Police Court on 26 May 1926 to answer several summonses under the Emergency Powers Act of 1926. These, according to *The Times*, included "doing an act calculated to cause disaffection among the civilian population; failing to notify under the Aliens Act of 1920 his change of occupation and, being an alien, attempting to promote industrial unrest in an industry which he himself had not been engaged in for the preceding two years". This case arose in connection with a dispute between two master bakers, Bolor and Kossoff, and their employees. The magistrate was clearly particularly ill disposed towards Prooth, not least, it would seem, because he was an alien. The defence argued that the offences were trivial and that the defendant's real crime appeared to be that that he was a foreigner and a communist, neither of which was an offence even in a court of law. The magistrate was not impressed by such arguments, and said, "Englishmen's troubles were their own and did not require men to come from Russia or other countries and set themselves up with the information and brain of those countries to foment discontent among Englishmen, who otherwise, would be working peaceably". Prooth was sentenced to five months hard labour with a recommendation for his deportation. The reporter and the editor of the *East London Advertiser* expressed almost venomous satisfaction at the severity of the sentence imposed, and described Prooth variously as "a communist agitator", "a paid agent of Moscow" and as "a supporter of the Labour Party in Mile End".

Prooth was tried alongside Dan Frankel, a member of Stepney Borough Council, chairman of Stepney Trades Council and the Stepney Council of Action set up during the general strike. Frankel, who was a longstanding councillor and well-known in the Stepney labour movement was fined at the same time £25 and 5 guineas costs. Both Prooth and Frankel were sentenced for committing an act calculated to injure or prevent the proper use or working of the shop and factory of Israel Kossoff by threatening to cause the electric power to be withdrawn contrary to the Electricity Regulations. After his release Prooth was deported. Non-Jewish master bakers in London were also delighted by the firm attitude of the judicial bench and of the Jewish Master Bakers' Association. They praised the patience and forbearance of the Jewish master bakers who were now reaping the reward of firmness, and urged them not to use the union label and to employ whom they pleased.

The London District of the AUOB was weakened by the general strike, but the Jewish Bakers' Union was not adversely affected. At the end of 1925 its membership was 102, a year later it was 104 and by the end of 1929 it had risen to 125. Nonetheless, the 1920s were a period of instability and uncertainty for the union, especially at the top. I. Sharp retired towards the end of 1924. He was replaced by Prooth, who was deported to Russia after the general strike. L. Brenner took over as secretary but was found guilty of misappropriation of funds. He was followed by a stop-gap secretary, M. Faulck. Faulck was succeeded by H. Wilson. Shortly thereafter, Wilson was convicted of forgery and imprisoned. Only when Solomon Lever took over was stability restored. The union's finances had been in a parlous state during this period, and the annual returns submitted by Lever at the end of 1929 were described as "the best possible under difficult circumstances". However, the returns also stated that the recommendations of an investigating committee had been carried out, so that generally the books and the affairs of the union "are now in order".

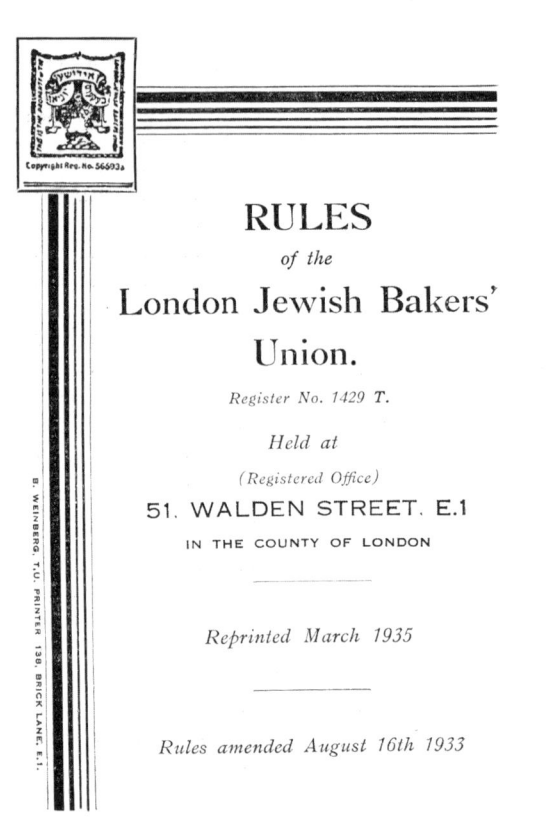

English-language cover of the LJBU rule book 1933
Reproduced by permission of the Jewish Museum, London

Chapter 12. The Rule Book of 1933

Under Lever's stewardship, the administration of the union as a whole was put "in order". Revised union rules were published in English and in Yiddish in 1933 — by that time the younger members of the union were English-speaking, and some had little or no knowledge of Yiddish. There is a gap in the union's own records of its activities covering almost a quarter of a century. However, from 1939 onwards minutes were kept in English. Neither minutes prior to 1939, nor the earliest rules of the union seem to be extant. These had at one time been lodged with the Registry of Friendly Societies, then, after the 1971 Industrial Relations Act, they were handed over to the Registry of Trade Union and Employers' Associations. Following the Act's repeal, the original rules of the union and its financial returns from 1951 onwards were supposedly sent to the Public Records Office, but they have proved untraceable.

According to the Annual Financial Return of 1912, the rules were altered on 29 April 1910, but again no copy can be traced. A copy of the rules as printed in August 1933 still exists — these rules remained largely unchanged throughout the rest of the union's existence. It is clear from the certificate of registration that the union had completely rewritten its rules — presumably in line with changing circumstances.

This rule book, printed in Yiddish and in English, is not only interesting for what it included, but also for what it excluded. Unlike many unions, the London Jewish Bakers' Union claimed no long term political objective — such as socialism or a cooperative system, despite the union's early attempts to form cooperatives. This may have been a consequence of the nature of the trade itself. Generally, Jewish bakers had only a few employees, who all worked alongside the employer. As Morris Cohen and J. Middleburgh explained, the ambitious worker would often open his own bakery. When that enterprise failed, he would be plunged once more into the ranks of the workers. In a small scale industry where the worker looked forward to being his own boss, the lack of any socialist objective is hardly surprising.

The objectives of the union were narrow but no different in essence from those of other unions — to protect their members in relation to their trade as follows:

a) To regulate the relations between employers and employed.
b) To reduce the hours of labour for a working week to 48 hours.

[This was certainly a considerable advance on the objectives of the union up till the outbreak of the First World War. At best a 54 or 60 hour week would have been the ambition of the LJBU and the AUOB.]

c) To establish a Central Fund for the protection of the members and advancement of wages.

d) To achieve the total abolition of overtime.

e) To use all legitimate means for the moral, social, educational and economic advancement of its members.

f) To support its members in sickness.

g) To give payment of a benefit on the death of a member or his wife, and to assist members in distress.

h) To persuade all operatives working at the Baking Trade to join the union and to refuse to work with non-unionists when all reasonable arguments failed.

i) To federate with other Trade Unions having similar objectives.

Another objective in the rules, dear to the hearts of the membership, was the use of a trade union label to show that loaves had been baked by trade unionists and under trade union conditions. The union had waged many struggles over the years around that issue.

The section of the rules concerning disputes contained a unique feature, which surely no other union has ever laid down, or been in a position to enforce: where unionised employees of a bakery could not themselves settle a dispute, and where the officers of the union decided that the members deserve support, "the employer shall be asked to attend the Committee of the union to try and bring the matter to a friendly conclusion". Needless to say, employers did not always comply with this union rule!

Like most unions, the London Jewish Bakers' Union was concerned with education and with the welfare of its members. Points (e), (f) and (g) were important features of the union's work, especially given the rudimentary welfare system before World War 2. On sick pay it declared that members on "the Sick Fund shall receive 15s. per week or 2/6 per day. A member is entitled to 12 weeks pay". Rule 14 determined that "in the event of the decease of a member his nominee shall receive the sum of £10 which shall be collected by a levy of 2s. on all members". In the event of the death of a member's wife "the member shall receive the sum of £5 which shall be collected by a levy on all members of 1s." From the beginning of 1933 there was also a distress fund for "the purpose of helping such members who, in the opinion of the Management Committee, are in distress". The rules stipulated that "every member in the union shall subscribe 1s. per quarter for the maintenance of this fund". The union minutes recorded the assistance given with sick pay, death benefit, and the distress fund drawn upon to help members and their families in need.

Yiddish-language cover of the 1933 LJBU rule book
Reproduced by permission of the Jewish Museum, London

Chapter 13. 1940-1969: Decline and Fall?

In the 1930s membership was stable at around 120, but the war brought problems and a fall in membership. Many members joined the forces or left London to avoid the bombing. By October 1940 there were only about 40 paying members, although the annual return claimed a membership of 75, and the union affiliation to the Trade Union Congress was still 110. A members' meeting in that month took emergency measures. It reduced the secretary's salary, vacated the Walden Street premises, and hired a room in the Workers Circle building, in Great Alie Street, not far from there. (The Workers Circle was a Friendly Society of Jewish workers whose members were mainly immigrants or the children of immigrants).[1] No meetings were held after this date until April 1942, when two took place. Membership was then only 60 because of the evacuation and call-up. On, of all days, May Day 1942, the minutes recorded that because of the shortage of labour the employers were engaging non-union men, and it was clear that the union in its weak state could do little or nothing to prevent this. In October 1943 the AUOB had proposed that the Jewish Bakers amalgamate with them, but the union decided against, and the following month it moved to new offices at Adler Hall. The union remained there until 1947, when it was given notice to quit by the United Synagogue.

Not till January 1946 did the minutes strike a note of optimism. At this stage membership was 70, according to the annual return, and the funds of the union had reached £200. In 1947 the union felt sufficiently strong to warn the master bakers that action would be taken against their employing non-union labour. This was necessary, given the unemployment existing among the union membership. Membership rose slowly but steadily to over 100 by 1950, but after that a gradual decline again set in. In 1956 the union, despite its declining membership, secured an agreement from the Jewish master bakers to pay four days' wages in lieu of holidays lost when Jewish Holy Days fell on the Sabbath. The same year the union displayed its solidarity by agreeing to help the AUOB to recruit the pastry cooks in Jewish bakeries – the Jewish union did not organise pastry cooks.

The End of an Epoch

In 1959 the union made the headlines in the national and local press in an episode which shocked both its membership and the

East End of London. It almost certainly contributed to the eventual collapse of the union by removing a key figure, Solomon Lever, the union secretary, a man both locally respected and fairly well known in national trade union and Jewish circles. The event was described in the *Jewish Chronicle* under the heading "Secretary lured to Death".[2] Lever, who was also acting general secretary of the Workers Circle Friendly Society and lived in Hackney, got a bogus telephone call claiming that there was a fire in the building next to the Friendly Society's office and that a police car and a detective would call to remove any money to a place of safety. When they arrived at the building Lever was bound, gagged and left in the car while the thieves, using Lever's keys, entered the office and robbed the safe. Lever died of heart failure and his body was dumped in Epping Forest near Chingford. The money stolen belonged to the Friendly Society. Solomon Lever had been born in Poland and brought to England as a child. He had risen to become the Mayor of Hackney. He had attended over twenty trade union congresses as the delegate from the Jewish Bakers' Union, and had distinguished himself by his forthright and courageous contributions on the renewal of fascist activities in England and the dangers of German rearmament.

Amalgamation ... Collapse

Back in 1943 the Jewish bakers had declined a proposal that they amalgamate with the AUOB. By the beginning of 1960, the Jewish bakers' continued decline in membership — it was then 57 — necessitated drastic measures. The union, which no longer had a full-time secretary, sought advice from Jacob Fine, a long-serving officer of the tailors' union in East London. His view was that, unless the present membership was prepared to throw its full weight into sustaining its independence, the union would either have to close or amalgamate with the AUOB. In the latter case, the Jewish bakers would constitute a separate branch and would maintain their traditions and customs. In March 1960 Fine reported that he had had a most sympathetic interview with Vic Feather at the TUC on the question of amalgamation. Feather then contacted Mr. Halliday, secretary of the AUOB, and it was agreed that, if negotiations were successful, the Jewish bakers would become the AUOB London Jewish Bakers' Branch.

Lengthy discussions ensued in the committee concerning suitable terms of affiliation. In July 1960 an understanding was reached between Mr. Haynes of the AUOB and Fine, representing the Jewish Bakers' Union, that : "the Amalgamated Union will continue to recognise the customs and agreements of the Jewish baking fraternity as operating in orthodox Jewish bakers' establishments" and that "the Amalgamated Union would not send its members to such establishments (i.e. orthodox Jewish bakeries) on Friday nights."

Interviewed in the *Daily Worker* in December 1960, Morris Cohen spoke in favour of amalgamation: "You see, there is no future ... the average age of the members is over fifty ... some over seventy... quite a lot are grandfathers like me ... and there are no youngsters coming into the industry..." The Jewish population of East London had been scattered since the Blitz, and the new generation "did not readily acquire the taste for chollahs and rye bread" There were barely a dozen Jewish bakeries in all London. Cohen continued: "the few we have are great craftsmen ... no mass production ... I wrote to the late Gilbert Harding when he was complaining he couldn't eat mass produced bread these days ... explained how we made bread." However, in the membership ballot at the end of January 1961, 26 members opposed amalgamation and only 14 voted in favour. Despite its small and declining membership, the majority deeply cherished the long independence of their union, and took pride in being the only Jewish union outside Israel. They believed that as the last remnant of an independent union of Jewish workers, everything possible had to be done to revitalise the union. One step was for the union to participate in Jewish social life.

There were numerous discussions on how to increase union membership. In April 1960 Fine suggested granting an amnesty to all old members, allowing them to rejoin the union as new members, without having to pay their arrears. This reflects the desperate situation of the union — in "the good old days" such a suggestion would have been rejected immediately as a disgraceful departure from trade union principles. It was becoming clear that there was little scope for increasing membership, but in March 1961 Fine suggested that at least something could be done to safeguard the position of the remaining members. It was decided to update the rules and to prepare and agreement with each employer stipulating claims and privileges of union members. Fine also suggested that the Jewish bakers affiliate to the Jewish Board of Deputies and to the World Jewish Congress, so that the voice of the union could be heard, but the Board of Deputies no longer accepted trade union affiliations.

By May 1963 the union was so enfeebled that some members proposed to dissolve it. In response, Fine appealed to those present to go all out to inject new life into the union. Although it was difficult to carry on without an active committee, Fine hoped that if negotiations were resumed with the master bakers and a third week's holiday was won, this would provide an incentive for all members to play a greater part in the running of the union. Despite this appeal the work of the union and the spirit of its membership continued to flag. No further meeting was held till September, when the chairman, Morris Cohen, proposed that with no working committee and an indifferent membership, the union should close down. However Fine, although almost 80 years old, was still imbued with a fighting spirit, for he urged yet again all present not to give up the struggle to maintain the union. The secretary, Miss Ray Brooks, pointed out that a vote for the dissolution of the union could not be taken at that meeting, as the rules required that two-thirds of the members should be in attendance to take such a step. In October 1963 Cohen suggested that, to attract new members, sick benefits should be raised from £1 to £1 10s for 13 weeks, and this was unanimously agreed at the November meeting. At the same committee meeting Mr. Sylvester pointed out that the members in his baker's shop were scattered throughout London. As it was inconvenient for them to come to the union to pay contributions, and this was likely to place them in arrears, he volunteered to collect union dues from them. This was welcomed. It is clear that one of the reasons for poor attendance at union meetings and decline in membership was that members were no longer concentrated in the Whitechapel area but were dispersed throughout Greater London.

The last recorded meeting of the union was dated 29 May 1964. Its membership was then 32.[3] The members met, more or less socially, at intervals.[4] The union lingered on, its membership continuing to decline — at the end of 1964 it had 28 members, in 1966 24, in 1968 and 1969 a round — not even a baker's — dozen![5]

After the Second World War the East End of London ceased to be a centre of British Jewry. British Jews were becoming increasingly assimilated into the non-Jewish British population. The dispersal of East London Jewry (beginning even before the Second World War) would in itself eventually have led to the collapse of the union. But in addition, the younger English speaking Jewish population was no longer cemented together by the use of the Yiddish language and by fears of anti-Semitism.

Additionally, the baking industry was becoming increasingly dependent on machinery. Small bakeries had given way to the large highly automated chain bakeries, which required no special "Jewish" skills to produce the product. And so, without the need or the base for an exclusively Jewish union, the London Jewish Bakers' Union came to an end, and with it the end of a chapter in trade union history.

The banner of the London Jewish Bakers' Union
Reproduction courtesy of the Jewish Museum, London

Chapter 14. Conditions of Work from 1939 Onwards

The weekly meetings of the union committee were recorded in the minutes, as were the members' meetings, held quarterly and on special occasions where the committee thought this appropriate. Meetings were more irregular during the war, and in the latter years of the union as its membership declined, so too did its frequency of meetings. These minutes, covering the quarter of a century from 1939, give us a fuller picture of the working conditions, wages, hours and holidays, of the bakers in the Jewish union. In addition the problems facing the union come to life more vividly than in the minutes of most trade union bodies.

Wages

We do not know whether a specific scale of wages to members of the London Jewish Bakers' Union was laid down by the union or paid by the employers in the period after the First World War. There may be information on this in the records of the London Jewish Master Bakers' Protection Society, but these were inaccessible. Mr. H. Grodzinski wrote to me on behalf of the society in 1974 stating that most Jewish bakers got higher wages than their non-Jewish counterparts in the early 1900s.[1] This situation continued, not least because bread baked for Jewish customers is "more of a 'home made' type and is different from the ordinary English loaf". There is some evidence that does indicate this.

Nonetheless, there are individual pieces of evidence indicating the sort of wages obtaining in the industry at certain times. In February 1939 a union member was censured for working at Kossoff's bakery below the minimum rate. It would appear that on one day he received 15s. for 10 hours work, and in the following week the same sum of money for 12 hours. Assuming that it was the latter situation which raised objections, this would mean that an experienced baker would receive £4 10s. per week for a 6-day week, which was then common, plus overtime rate for Sunday work. Given the prices and general conditions of the time, such wages might have sufficed for a satisfactory standard of living.

In April 1939 a conference between the Jewish Master Bakers and the London Jewish Bakers' Union agreed that, in connection with the forthcoming Trade Board for the Baking Industry, the Ministry of Labour should be approached to recognise 1s. 6d per hour as the minimum rate for table hands and 2s. for foremen.

Moreover the Jewish bakers had the advantage of being paid double time for Sundays, even though they were working in lieu of Saturday when they could not be employed anyway. Minimum trade board rates were introduced at the beginning of September 1939, the month when war broke out, but what the actual rates were is unclear. In particular the union minutes suggest that foremen were only receiving something between 1s. 6d and 2s. Some employers were not always paying the minimum rates, but by 1944 members were definitely in receipt of wages far above Trade Board rates.

On 26 April 1951 the minutes recorded a member's complaint that he was receiving only £4 16s. for 3 days from his employers (Grodzinski's) instead of the £7 for 3 days he had been given for the previous 5 weeks. This would mean that for a six-day week the rate of pay was £14, plus overtime for Sunday work. This was more than three times the rates paid in 1939. Even accounting for inflation this was an improvement in wages.

Hours of work

In May 1939 a member was censured for working more than 11 hours per day. It is clear from this that the working day had improved little, if at all, in over three decades since the establishment of the union. However, while the working day was longer than average, the union was determined to ensure that excessive hours were not worked. Twice in the following months stern warnings were issued against working overtime. The union also employed committee members to keep a watch on bakeries where there was any suspicion of overtime working.

Shortly after the outbreak of the Second World War the committee decided that a 48-hour week must be instituted, and a special meeting of union members was called in November 1939 to explain the need to limit hours. It was discovered that one bakery had been working a 70-hour week. The 48-hour week was vital as a means of reducing unemployment. The committee resolved that unemployed members must be given jobs once every 2 weeks (prior to this it tried to ensure that a job was given once every 3 weeks). This system, operated by the London Jewish Bakers' Union, was known as the "credential system," On more than one occasion the minutes recorded that members who did not play their part in "giving a job" under the credential system were given stern warning of disciplinary action. At the end of November 1939 both employers' and workers' organisations agreed a 48-hour week must be instituted, with special additional payment for night work (10% extra) and for overtime (time and a half or time and a quarter), although this agreement was often breached and employers had to be warned not to exceed the 48-hour week. At the same time, members were expected not to leave their employment without permission. This was to ensure that immediately a baker left his job another worker could step in, so that members who were unemployed would benefit. On the other hand in July 1940 when an unemployed member was given a credential to fill a job for a particular occasion (e.g. in the co-operative bakery in an Amalgamated Union shop) and did not turn up, this too was the occasion for reproof, because it reflected on the good faith of the Jewish Bakers' Union.

There was no further reference to the credential system for the rest of the war, which would suggest that this was not necessary, but the system reappeared in 1946. However, in May 1950 the minutes noted that the union had five unemployed members and that this small number did not justify the reinstitution of the credential system. There was no further mention of the credential system.

Night-work

At a time when customers wanted bread at its freshest — and when unlike today there were no special ingredients for preserving freshness — it was taken for granted that bakers should work throughout the night to enable the housewife to buy newly baked bread in the early morning. The first reference to night work in the minutes was in September 1940, because members felt uneasy at being called to work at night during air raids. Night-work was looked upon as normal, if not acceptable. The campaign against night working in the baking industry only began once the war against Germany was over. On 27 July 1945 Mr. Halliday of the AUOB London District spoke at a meeting of the Jewish Bakers on his union's efforts to abolish night-work, which he pledged to intensify. By April 1946 the Jewish bakers were ready to work alongside the AUOB to end night-work and even, if need be, to take strike action. Six months later the AUOB General Secretary again addressed the London Jewish Bakers' Union on the same topic, and praised the Jewish bakers for their high degree of organisation.

By March 1949 the AUOB had made a film on abolishing night-working, and in June representatives of the London Jewish Bakers' Union met with the Jewish Master Bakers to discuss the effect the abolition of night-work would have on the Jewish baking industry. The matter dragged on. In October 1950 it was agreed that another conference be held between Jewish employers and workers. Early in 1951 the Jewish bakers replied to a letter from the Ministry of Labour, expressing their firm and unanimous support of the efforts of the English and Scottish Trade Unions efforts to abolish night-baking. Almost exactly one year afterwards the Jewish bakers told their employers that they were prepared to work one night only a week, on a Saturday. The issue remained unsettled and in June 1953 the union tried to enlist the support of the local MPs Butler, Edwards and Orbach. In February 1954 the AUOB general secretary informed the London Jewish Bakers' Union that the Jewish Master Bakers' Protection Society were submitting a case for two nights a week work to the parliamentary committee. The AUOB pledged support for only one night's work a week.

More than three years later the matter remained unresolved, for in September 1957 the Provincial Jewish Master Bakers wanted night-baking to be agreed for Thursday and Saturday and day-work for the rest of the week. The London Jewish Bakers' Union assured the AUOB secretary, who had raised the matter with Solomon Lever at the TUC in Blackpool, that his members unanimously supported the provisions of the Parliament Bill, which did not permit more than one night a week for night-baking, and that they were wholeheartedly in favour of abolishing night baking entirely. At last, in February 1958, the Hours of Work Bill brought about a changeover from night- to day-time baking.

Holidays

With regard to holidays the Jewish Bakers Union was in a unique position. The day of rest unquestionably had to be the Sabbath. No work could be undertaken from Friday nightfall till Saturday nightfall. This did not preclude work on Saturday night once the Sabbath was at an end. At a time when there were only statutory holidays for most workers, the Jewish bakers did not have to work on Jewish holydays (New Year — 2 days; Day of Atonement — 1 day; Shevuoth — 2 days; Succoth — 4 days; Pesach — 8 days), though they might well be expected to do so on national holidays like Christmas. As the eight days of Pesach (Passover) were a period when no bread was to be eaten (matzos took its place) this was an enforced holiday. It could be a mixed blessing, as it would be an unusual employer who would be prepared to pay for this time off.

Consequently, for religious reasons, in the early years of the 20th century Jewish bakers enjoyed more days holiday than their non-Jewish colleagues. The question of holidays was probably not an important issue before the First World War, and it did not loom large until after the Second World War, when the union was already declining. Holidays were first mentioned in the minutes in June 1949, which noted a meeting between the employers and the union representatives. One matter discussed was: "the question of 2 weeks holiday with pay, counting the Passover week as one of them". In August 1953 the union secretary approached the employers on the question of Yom Kippur (the day of Atonement), a holiday which that year fell on Friday night and the Saturday. As the prevailing custom in British industry was that a day lost from statutory holidays was made up by an extra day's holiday at a later date, he argued that the same right should be accorded to the Jewish bakers when a Jewish holiday was in effect lost because it fell on a Saturday. In June 1955, nearly two years after this matter was first raised, a special members' meeting was called to discuss how to secure a day's holiday in lieu of any Jewish holiday lost because the holiday fell on the Sabbath. The employers' representatives were willing to concede, but the employers rejected their own representatives' recommendation. In response, the union decided to give the employers notice that its members would not work on the night of Saturday 18 June. The employers backed down on the day's holiday in question, and proposed that the issue in principle be settled by arbitration. The union members agreed to the proposal.

Five months later the union expressed solidarity with the AUOB members working for Grodzinski's, a leading Jewish bakery, which was not prepared to give pay in lieu of Jewish holidays. The outcome of this dispute was not recorded. At the end of March 1962 a special members' meeting was held to hear Morris Cohen report on discussions the union had held with Mr. Halliday of the AUOB. The points that emerged are worth quoting in detail for the light they shed on questions of wages, hours and holidays:

> 1) On the National Union's Charter there are provisions for a £12 minimum weekly rate, a 40 hour working week, and 3 weeks summer holidays. But, said the chairman, these provisions are in the Charter only and not in practice. In point of fact, said the Chairman, according to Mr. Halliday's own statement, only the co-op and some federated shops have a 42 hour week. In all other shops 44 hours is the normal practice.

2) The National Union had, in fact, made an application to the Federation for a third week's summer holiday, but the union had eventually withdrawn its application in favour of a demand for a pay rise of £1 a week.

3) The National Union had recently submitted to the Wages Council a proposal for a 42 hour week, but this proposal, according to Mr. Halliday, was opposed by the independent members of the Wages Council, and the matter had therefore, been postponed for 6 months.

4) With regard to our Union's present negotiations with the Jewish Master Bakers, Mr. Halliday advised that the Union should go forward with the demand for 2 weeks summer holiday exclusive of Passover, and should not submit the alternative of a wage rise. This, said Mr. Halliday, can safely be left pending the outcome of his Union's negotiations on a national level.

5) Mr. Halliday strongly advised that our Union should intimate to our employers our intention to terminate the existing practice of recognising the Passover week as a summer holiday, and to demand a properly negotiated agreement, which should stabilise not only the summer holidays but also the working hours and the basic rates. This, said the chairman, is the gist of the interview with Mr. Halliday.

The meeting unanimously resolved to instruct the committee to go forward with the demand for 3 weeks summer holiday. If the employers refused, the union would formally notify the Master Bakers' Association of its intention to cease recognising Passover week as summer holiday and that a new agreement should be negotiated to cover the holiday periods. Eventually in November 1963 the masters conceded the extra week's holiday in summer providing the union was prepared to forgo the day off in lieu when a Jewish holiday fell on the Sabbath.

Complaints and problems

The union was ever conscious of the need to preserve its high reputation, and was often called upon to act as adjudicator in quarrels between fellow members. In an industry where men worked long hours in trying conditions, it was not surprising that tempers should sometimes be frayed and that harsh words or even blows be exchanged.

It was also customary for union representatives to visit members in distress or sickness, and for that matter, on "simchas", joyous occasions. One such a simcha — a wedding presentation in 1939 —

was obviously not as enjoyable as the union representative Mr. L. would have wished. His dignity was keenly affronted because, out of all the guests, he alone was not given a drink. The committee was clearly in sympathy. It formally passed an expression of regret at the treatment shown to its representative.

On another occasion, in 1940, the minutes dealt in detail with a dispute between one of its members, Mr. R, and Mr. K. of the Tailors' and Garment Workers' Union, who had been playing dominoes in a hall – probably Circle House. It appears that the game of dominoes can spark off violence as deadly as a game of cards or a political dispute! Poor Mr. K. was so badly hurt — he had three ribs fractured — by Mr. R. that he was off work for some time. Mr. R. was fined, warned against such unbecoming conduct and removed from the union committee.

Violent conflicts between employer and employee within bakeries occasionally occurred. In February 1946 the union was asked to intervene so that one employee could be given work elsewhere, for otherwise: "There would certainly be a tragedy". In 1950, in an incident of "unbrotherly relations" between 4 members employed in Bernstein's bakery, the union had to intercede to save 2 members from being dismissed. Again, in 1952, when quarrels between members in a bakery became extremely acrimonious, the union warned the two members involved that unless their relationship improved one would have to go.

The minutes also recorded occasional complaints of "poaching" of members by the AUOB. (No doubt that union sometimes levelled similar charges against the London Jewish Bakers' Union). However, these differences were usually settled amicably. The union was quick to act when there was any question of non-union labour being employed. It is interesting to note that, especially after the Second World War, non-Jewish workers were engaged in the Jewish baking industry and were accepted without question by the London Jewish Bakers' Union (unless they were already AUOB members, in which case they would not have been accepted as this would have been regarded as poaching).

Solidarity

While the first call upon the union's help was obviously from its own members, the Jewish bakers were ready to contribute generously to causes they considered deserving. In general they worked in harmony with the AUOB, and often came to each other's support, for example on questions of holidays, night-work, rates of pay, etc. The calls upon the union funds were such, indeed, that on more than one occasion it had to raise union fees, so that its normal union commitments, as well as special grants for accidents to its members, to the sick, and to the unemployed, could be met — otherwise, as the minutes put it, the union funds could "dwindle away to nothing."

Before the Second World War, anti-Semitism in England and abroad was a major concern. In March 1939 for example, the membership was called upon to bear a special levy of 2s. per head, so that the Jewish People's Council, a body which struggled against Mosleyism and creeping fascism in this country, could continue to wage its campaigns. The situation of their Jewish brethren in Palestine obviously was not far from their minds, and in April 1942 the union sent a donation of two guineas to the Friends of Jewish Labour in Palestine. During the war considerable help was sent to the Soviet Red Cross – for example, in February 1943 it was agreed to levy 5s. per member for this purpose. In 1948, as the state of Israel was coming into existence, the union agreed a £1 levy on all members for Palestine Histadruth (the Jewish Trade Union movement in Palestine). This was a period of intense feeling among the Jewish community about the situation in Palestine. The union sent further donations of £100 to Israel in 1951 and to the Joint Palestine Appeal in 1952.

At the beginning of 1949 the union applied for affiliation to the national Labour Party, and in 1951 it contributed £10 to assist the Labour Party, to augment its election fund and to assure the return of a Labour Government. Other examples of solidarity include a donation in 1950 of £5 5s. to the tobacco workers' strike fund.

Appendix. In a Jewish Bakery

(*Most of the information in this chapter I have gleaned from parents, grandmother, Mr. Cohen and Mr. Middleburgh*)

It is impossible to write a book or pamphlet on Jewish bakers without mentioning certain characteristically different types of Jewish bread and rolls. If there is one outstanding and supreme Jewish contribution to the world of baking it is the chollah, a braided loaf of white bread glazed with egg white. It is as Leo Rosten, the famed American writer considers, in his book *The Joys of Yiddish*, "a bread to rank with the most exquisite production of the baker's art". This "food for angels" is normally reserved for Sabbath and festivals — at other times, till recently, it was customary for Jewish people to eat "black" bread or "brown" (rye) bread. On holidays it is kneaded into other shapes, round, ladderlike etc. On the Jewish New Year it is round to symbolise the fullness of the year to come, and on the festival known as Purim it is filled with raisins making it more than ever like cake in taste. On Friday night, the eve of the Sabbath, it is customary for religious Jews to place two chollahs on the table and, after a blessing is said, each member of the family is given a piece, and the meal is then eaten. The two chollahs are a reminder of the double portion of manna dropped by God on Friday (Sabbath being a day of rest) for the Jews wandering in the wilderness after fleeing from Egypt. Mr. Middleburgh recalled a custom, observed at least up to the Second World War. A very religious woman would come into the bakery, take a piece of chollah and throw it into the oven or fire as a burnt offering for the Sabbath.

Rye bread and black bread are more like the loaves we see here normally except that caraway seed is usually put into rye bread, and both black and brown bread have a characteristically sour flavour and are far more solid and satisfying than white bread.

Bagels

The origin of this word has been much disputed. According to Leo Rosten it is derived from the German "Beugel" — a round loaf of bread. Made of white flour and shaped like a doughnut, bagels must be placed into boiling water and boiled for about two minutes before being glazed with egg white. They are a rich shiny brown when ready to eat, and are as delicious to eat as to look at — second only in taste, texture and appearance to the chollah! Apparently they were round in shape because Jews considered the circular shape lucky

— God, who was perfect, chose the circle as the basic form in constructing the universe. (The Greeks thought the circle the perfect form because it had neither beginning nor end.) It is customary still in Jewish homes after a funeral to serve bagels and hard-boiled eggs. These are a symbol of the unending cycle of life and the world.

Platzels

These are made of white flour, kneaded into a ball. There is dimple in the centre (made if baked in the home by pressing two fingers into the centre). Platzels are usually garnished with poppy seeds or sesame seeds or with pieces of chopped onion.

Cholent

As religious Jews are not permitted to cook on the Sabbath (cooking being regarded as a form of work and all work is strictly forbidden on the day of rest), meals are prepared in advance and, where appropriate, may be kept in a hot oven. Perhaps the favourite midday meal on the Sabbath was cholent (it is not well known among younger Jews today). Its flavour improved, rather than suffered, by long slow cooking. Main ingredients — and there are a multitude of variations — are meat, potatoes, beans, onions, fat, flour. Once ready the heavy saucepan, filled to capacity and generously swathed in brown paper (or even newspaper), partly for safety, and partly to ensure that all the goodness was retained, would be carried on Friday before nightfall to the local baker's oven. The fires were banked but retained their heat overnight. Three or four old pence (dependent on the size of the saucepan) would be paid to the baker who would affix a ticket to the saucepan. The next day at midday a horde of children would turn up to carry home in triumph the precious container. Everyone was impatient for their own saucepan to be withdrawn. Many a time the ticket had fallen off or was so discoloured by baking as to be unreadable, and it was not infrequently the case that a saucepan was taken home only for it to be realised that it was not the right one, (and of course no one's cholent was as good as one's own) — then indeed there was a great "to do", while a hasty journey had to be made to make the appropriate exchange. Fortunately no one ever failed eventually to recover his own cherished dish.

Notes

Chapter 1

1. See for example (i) booklist issued by the Jewish Memorial Council and Central Council for Jewish Religious Education; (ii) Transactions of the Jewish Historical Society; (iii) Publications of the Wiener Library.
2. *Jewish Encyclopaedia* 1906, p. 216, vol. 12.
3. Annual Report, London Trades Council, 1907.
4. *National Reformer & Manx Weekly Review.* 3 and 24 April 1847.
5. *Reynolds Political Instructor,* 19 January 1850.
6. *The Working Man,* 7 April 1866.
7. *The Working Man,* 21 April 1866.

Chapter 2

1. P. Elman *Beginnings of the Jewish Trade Union Movement in England* (Transactions of the Jewish Historical Society XVIII, pp.53-62).
2. V. L.Lipman *Social History of the Jews in England 1850-1950* p.116.
3. Annual Reports 1909 of GFTU and LTC.
4. Letter from Mr Grodzinski 5 February 1974.
5. *Journeymen Bakers Magazine (JBM)* June 1888.
6. *JBM,* June 1888
7. *Arbeter Fraynd,* 18 May 1888.
8. *JBM* August 1888.
9. *JBM* December 1888.
10. *JBM* November 1889.
11. *JBM* December 1889.
12. *Jewish Chronicle (JC)* 1 November 1889.
13. *JBM* March 1890.
14. *JC* 16 January 1891.

Chapter 3

1. *JBM* August 1893.
2. *Reynolds News* 9 July 1893.
3. *Reynolds News* 10 September 1893
4. *JC* September 1893.
5. *JC* 15 September 1893
6. *JC* 22 September 1893.

7. *JC* 6 October 1893.
8. *JBM* September 1893.
9. *JBM* December 1893.
10. *JBM* April 1896.
11. *Westminster Gazette* 18 September 1894.
12. *Jewish World* 5 October 1894.
13. *JC* 8 January 1897.
14. *JC* 29 January 1897.
15. *JC* 26 February 1897.
16. *JC* 23 April 1897.
17. *JC* 24 September 1897.
18. *JC* 3 December 1897.
19. *JC* 7 January 1898.

Chapter 4

1. *JBM* August 1896.
2. *JC* 21 August 1896.
3. *JC* 28 August 1896.
4. Lloyd P. Gartner: *The Jewish Immigrant in England 1870-1914*, (Detroit 1960) pp. 52-3.
5. *JBM* October 1896.
6. *JC* 9 October 1896.
7. *JC* 4 September 1896.
8. *JC* 23 October 1896.
9. *JC* 4 December 1896.
10. *JBM* January 1897.
11. *JC* 15 January 1897.
12 *JBM* February 1897.
13. *JC* 29 January 1897.
14. *JC* 15 July 1897
15. *JC* 20 August 1897.
16. *JC* 11 September 1897
17. *JBM* June 1901.
18. *JC* 3 May 1901.
19. *JC* 19 July 1901.
20. *JC* July-November 1901.
21. *JBM* September 1901.
22. *JBM* August 1901.
23. *JBM* September 1901.
24. *JBM* August 1902.
25. *JC* 12 December 1902.

Chapter 5

1. *JC* 9 October 1896.
2. *JC* 6 November 1896.
3. *JC* 22 January 1897.
4. *JC* 26 February 1897
5. *JC* 23 July 1897.
6. *Reynolds News* 4 September 1892.
7. *JC* 12 and 26 November 1897.
8. *JC* 7 January 1898.
9. *JBM* January 1898.
10. *JC* 6 October 1899.
11. *JC* 13 October 1899.
12. *JC* 29 December 1899.
13. *JC* 12 January 1900.
14. *JBM* May 1900.
15. *JC* 27 April 1900.
16. *JBM* June 1900.
17. Lloyd P. Gartner *op. Cit.*
18. J. R. Garrard *The Wiener Library Bulletin,* 1970, vol. 24.

Chapter 6

1. *JC* 25 January 1901
2. *JC* 26 April 1901.
2. *JC* 14 February 1902.
3. *JC* 17 October 1902.
4. *JC* 16 January 1903.
5. *JC* 30 January 1903.
6. JC 13 February 1903
7. *JC* 14 August 1903.
8. *JC* 18 September 1903.
9. *JC* 2 October 1903.
10. *JC* 16 October 1903.
11. *JC* 18 December 1903.

Chapter 7

1. *Reynolds News* 24 January 1904.
2. *Reynolds News* 20 March 1904.
3. *Reynolds News* 19 June 1904.
4. *Reynolds News* 27 March 1904.
5. *JC* 8 April 1904.

6. *Daily Express* 11 April 1904.
7. *Bakers Record* 15 April 1904.
8. *Reynolds News* 17 April 1904.
9. *Arbeter Fraynd* 15 April 1904.
10. *Arbeter Fraynd* 22 April 1904.
11. *Jewish World* 15 April 1904.
12. *Jewish World* 22 April 1904.
13. *JC* 29 April 1904..
14. *Bakers Record* 29 April 1904.
15. *JC* 20 May 1904.
16. *Arbeter Fraynd* 20 May 1904.
17. *JC* 3 June 1904.
18. *Arbeter Fraynd* 2 June 1904.
19. *JC* 17 June 1904.
20. *JBM* July 1904.
21. *JC* 24 June 1904.
22. *JBM* August 1904.
23. *Arbeter Fraynd* 8 July 1904.
24. *Naye Tsayt* 1 July 1904.
25. *JC* 24 June 1904, 8 July 1904.
26. *JC* 12 August 1904.
27. *JC* 24 June 1904.
28. *JC* 8 July 1904.
29. *JBM* February 1905.
30. *JC* 30 December 1904.
31. Rudolf Rocker, *The London Years*, pp. 170-171

Chapter 8

1. *The Times* 9 June 1904 (cited in K. W. Wedderburn's *Cases and Materials in Labour Law*. CUP 1967).
2. Noted in the *Jewish Year Book*, 1904.
3. *Social History of the Jews in England 1850-1950* p. 117.
4. Letter from Prof. Lord Wedderburn 3 June 1983.

Chapter 9

1. *JBM* February 1905.
2. *JC* 24 February 1905.
3. *JC* 9 June 1905.
4. *JBM* June 1905.
5. *JBM* July 1905.
6. *JBM* April 1906.

7. *JC* 28 July 1905.
8. *JC* 4 August 1905.
9. *JC* 1 September 1905.
10. *JC* 27 October 1905.
11. *JC* 19 January 1906.
12. *JC* 9 February 1906.
13. *JC* 2 March 1906.
14. *JC* 16 March 1906.
15. *JC* 6 April 1906.
16. *JC* 1 June 1906.
17. *JC* 17 August 1906.
18. *ibid*
19. *JC* 17 September 1906.
20. *East London Advertiser* 8, 15, 29 September, 6, 27 October 1906.
21. *JC* 28 September 1906.
22. *JC* 14 September 1906.
23. *JC* 28 September 1906.
24. *JC* 14 December 1906.
25. *JC* 16 August 1907.
26. *JC* 8 February 1907.
27. *JC* 16 August 1907.
28. *JC* 25 January 1907.
29. *JC* 5 April 1907.
30. *JC* 10 January 1908.
31. *JC* 1 May 1908.
32. *JBM* June 1909.
33. *JBM* July 1910.
34. *JBM* March 1911.
35. *JBM* April 1911.
36. *JBM* May-September 1911; GFTU Minutes May 1910; LTC minutes August 1910.
37. *JC* 10 June 1910.
38. *JC* 24 June 1910.
39. *JC* 1 July 1910.

Chapter 10

1. *JC* 5 July 1912.
2. *JC* 24 May 1912.
3. *JC* 27 December 1912.
4. *JC* 23 August 1912.
5. *JBM* Jan 1913.
6. *JBM* May 1913.

7. *JC* 25 April 1913.
8. *JBM* June 1913.
9. *JBM* July 1913.
10. *JC* 2 May 1913.
11. *JC* 9 May 1913.
12. *JC* 20 June 1913.
13. *JBM* August – October 1913.
14. *JC* 5 September 1913.
15. *JC* 3 October 1913.
16. *Annual Financial Return* 1913.
17. *ibid.*
18. *JC* 17 October 1913.
19. *JC* 31 October 1913.
20. *The Baker and Confectioner* 10 October 1913.

Chapter 11

1. *JBM* January, March, July 1914.
2. *JBM* October 1914.
3. *JBM* August 1914.
4. *JBM* September 1914.
5. Lloyd P. Gartner, *op.cit.*, pp. 139-140.
6. *Annual Returns* of London Jewish Bakers' Union
7. Letter from Mr H. Grodzinski 5 February 1974.
8. *JBM* September 1926.
9. *Daily Worker* December 1960.
10. *JC, East London Advertiser, East London Observer,* 29 May 1926.

Chapter 13

1. Sources for all this information: *Minutes of the LJBU* 17 October 1940 to 29 November 1963.
2. *Jewish Chronicle* 19 July 1959
3. TUC report figures
4. According to Messrs Cohen and Middleburgh
5. TUC report.

Chapter 14

1. Letter from Mr H. Grodzinski, 5 February 1974.

Suggested further reading

On East End Jewish radicalism:
William J Fishman, *East End Jewish Radicals 1875-1914*, Duckworth, London, 1995
Joe Jacobs, *Out of the Ghetto*, Phoenix, London, 1993
Rudolf Rocker, *The London Years*, Five Leaves Publications, Nottingham
Jerry White, *Rothschild Buildings: life in an East End tenement block 1887-1920*, Routledge, London, 1980

On conditions in the baking industry:
Edwin Dare, "Journeymen Bakers In Mid-Nineteenth Century East London" in *East London Record*, 14, 1991
Ian MacKay, "Bondage in the bakehouse? The strange case of the journeymen bakers 1840-1880", in Royden Harrison, Jonathan Zeitlin, (eds), *Divisions of Labour: Skilled Workers and Technological Change in Nineteenth Century England*, Harvester, Brighton, 1985, pp. 47-86.
Karl Marx, *Capital*, Vol. 1, Chapter 10, section 2

THE SOCIALIST HISTORY SOCIETY

The Socialist History Society was founded in 1992 and includes many leading Socialist and labour historians, both academic and amateur, in Britain and overseas. The SHS holds regular events, public meetings and one-off conferences, and contributes to current historical debates and controversies. The society produces a range of publications, including the journal *Socialist History*.

The SHS is the successor to the Communist Party History Group, established in 1946. The society is now independent of all political parties and groups. We are engaged in and seek to encourage historical studies from a Marxist and broadly-defined left perspective. We are concerned with every aspect of human history from early social formations to the present day and aim for a global reach.

We are particularly interested in the struggles of labour, women, progressive and peace movements throughout the world, as well as the movements and achievements of colonial peoples, black people, and other oppressed communities seeking justice, human dignity and liberation.

Each year we produce two issues of our journal *Socialist History*, one or two historical pamphlets in our *Occasional Papers* series, and members' newsletters. We hold a public lecture and debate in London five times per year. In addition, we organise occasional conferences, book-launch meetings, and joint events with other sympathetic groups.

Join the Socialist History Society!
Members receive all our serial publications for the year at no extra cost and regular mailings about our activities. Members can vote at our AGM and seek election to positions on the committee, and are encouraged to participate in other society activities.

Annual membership fees (renewable every January):
Full UK   £20.00
Concessionary UK   £14.00
Europe full   £25.00
Europe concessionary   £19.00
Rest of world full   £30.00
Rest of world concessionary   £24.00

For details of institutional subscriptions, please e-mail the treasurer on francis@socialisthistorysociety.co.uk .

To join the society for 2009, please send your name and address plus a cheque/PO payable to **Socialist History Society** to: SHS, 50 Elmfield Road, Balham, London SW17 8AL. Subscriptions can also be paid online.

Visit our websites on www.socialisthistorysociety.co.uk and www.socialist-history-journal.org.uk .

JEWISH SOCIALISTS' GROUP

The Jewish Socialists' Group is delighted to collaborate with the Socialist History Society in publishing this remarkable story, which opens a window on an aspect of Jewish history while setting it firmly in its social, political and economic context.

We have, from our origins in the 1970s, and, since 1985 through our magazine, *Jewish Socialist*, aimed to reclaim a "people's history" of the Jews which connects our historical experience to the struggles of other working people and the oppressed. This is an important element in our commitment to building the kind of socialism that will encourage minorities to express and develop their historical and cultural identities. Such histories as *Union Bread* are a crucial resource in this endeavour.

The Jewish Socialists' Group is socialist, diasporist and secularist.

As **socialists** we know that there can be no secure future for Jews, other minorities, working people and the unemployed under a system promoting private greed instead of meeting need. We campaign for social and economic justice locally, nationally and internationally. We are anti-capitalist and anti-imperialist. We work for a socialist solution to the Israel/Palestine conflict based on equality and self-determination for Israeli and Palestinian Jews and Arabs. As socialists we campaign actively against conservative forces in our own community.

As **diasporists** we reject the negative ideology of Zionism, which undermines diaspora communities by insisting on the centrality of Israel to Jewish life. As diasporists we oppose the way Zionism subordinates the political, economic and cultural needs of Jewish communities to the demands of the Israeli state. We support the right of Jewish communities to exist and flourish in security and harmony with other communities in the countries where they live.

As **secularists** we recognise that people express Jewish identity in different ways. We support pluralism in Jewish life and work especially to strengthen progressive, secular Jewish identities. We challenge our communal "leaders" when they attempt to confine Jewish identity solely within a religious or Zionist straitjacket.

The JSG is an open and democratic organisation which works and campaigns with other groups that share some or all of our aims. We welcome all individuals who agree to work for our political principles and to support our democratically agreed policies.

For more information visit www.jewishsocialist.org.uk, email jsg@jewishsocialist.org.uk or write to: Jewish Socialists' Group, BM3725, London WC1N 3XX.

Other SHS Occasional Papers for sale

25 Francis King, *The Narodniks in the Russian Revolution: Russia's Socialist-Revolutionaries in 1917*, £5.00
24 Paul Auerbach, Willie Thompson, *Is there No Alternative? Historical Problems of Socialist Economic Strategies*, £2.50
23 Jim Riordan, *The last British Comrade trained in Moscow: the Higher Party School 1961 - 1963* , £2.50
22 Gavin Bowd, *Comintern Cadre: The Passion of Allan Eaglesham*, £2.50
21 Lionel Munby, D Huw Owen, James Scannell, *Local History since 1945: England, Wales and Ireland*, £3.00
19 W Raymond Powell, *Keir Hardie in West Ham: "A Constituency with a Past"*, £2.50
18 Andrew Boyd, *Marx, Engels and the Irish*, £4.00
17 Linda Colley, *Another Making of the English Working Class: The Lash and the Imperial Soldiery*, £2.00
16 John Newsinger, *British Intervention and the Greek Revolution*, £2.75
14 Victor Kiernan, *Twenty Years of Europe: The Engels-Lafargue Correspondence*, £2.75
13 Andrew Boyd, *Jim Connell: The Man Who Wrote the Red Flag*, £3.50
12 Jim Fyrth, *An Indian Landscape 1944-1946*, £5.50
10 Jim Mortimer, *The Formation of the Labour Party - lessons for today*, £2.50
8 David Duncan, *Mutiny in the RAF: The Air Force Strikes of 1946*, £4.95

To order these and other SHS Occasional Papers online, please visit http://www.socialisthistorysociety.co.uk/shop.htm. These pamphlets can also be ordered by post within the UK — please send a cheque for the requisite amount (post free) payable to **Socialist History Society**, together with your name and address, to

SHS
50 Elmfield Road
London
SW17 8AL